Commanded to Preach

GEORGE CRAIG STEWART
MEMORIAL LECTURES

Commanded to Preach

by HENRY I. LOUTTIT

The Seabury Press   New York

ACKNOWLEDGMENTS

Grateful acknowledgment is made to the following publishers
and authors for permission to use copyrighted material from
the titles listed below:

Alec R. Allenson, Inc.—Reginald H. Fuller, *What Is Liturgical Preaching?* (London: S.C.M. Press, 1957. Distributed in U.S.A. by Allenson's, Naperville, Illinois.)

University of Notre Dame Press—Louis Bouyer, *Liturgical Piety*

Foreword

IN THE MID-THIRTIES the Rev. Frederick S. Fleming, D.D., Rector of Trinity Church, Wall Street, excited an uncommon amount of discussion in church circles when he called for a moratorium on preaching. Of course, nobody took him seriously but seminary professors of Homiletics.

Yet, in a strange way, circumstances have combined to produce almost a moratorium on preaching. The astonishing and heartening growth of the Family Service as the main service on Sunday in many parishes has for practical reasons reduced the time allowed for the sermon to a bare few minutes.

It used to be that preachers were warned not to preach more than twenty minutes. Now a preacher is fortunate if at the Family Service, the one attended by the most people, he has longer than ten minutes in which to proclaim the Gospel. Often these few minutes must be devoted strictly to instructional, informational, or catechetical matters.

Thus it happens that an earnest church member can go to church for years without ever hearing a "real" sermon that stirs his heart and excites his mind with the love and beauty and challenge and judgment of the Christian Gospel.

This little book by the Bishop of South Florida

focuses our attention on the eminent position the sermon must occupy in the life and worship of the Church. Contemporary ecclesiastical architects seem to have grasped this point. In many of the new churches one sees the pulpit on one side of the chancel and, balancing it, the baptismal font on the other side, both pointing to, and looking away from, the altar. The Sacrament of the Water and the Sacrament of the Word both draw their meaning from, and give meaning to, the Sacrament of the Altar. Each is indispensable to the other.

Everything that happens in a church on a Sunday morning is "communication." The way the service is read or sung, the vestments which are worn, the announcements which are made, the choral offerings of the singers—these and everything in and about the church communicate something about the way that particular congregation feels and responds to its understanding of the Gospel.

The many and obvious failures in Christian living on the part of all of us seem to say that our communication system today has been short-circuited. Architecture, liturgical action, vestments, and the rest cannot carry the full load of communicating the Gospel. The sermon is essential, and the best sermon is one that is illuminated by the Sacred Scriptures. Only the preacher who has saturated himself in the Scriptures will communicate the Gospel effectively, as Bishop Louttit forcefully points out.

This book is based upon the George Craig Stewart

Lectures in Homiletics given at Seabury-Western Theological Seminary. The Seminary is proud to send it forth.

CHARLES U. HARRIS, JR.
DEAN

PREFACE

THE ART of public speaking has long intrigued me. As a lad in elementary school, I was a regular attendant on Sunday mornings at the Episcopal Church of which I had been a member since infancy. Sunday evenings were spent not at an Episcopal Church youth gathering but at the evening service of the nearby Baptist Church, where a gifted preacher spoke. Frequently my father took my older brother and me to political rallies to hear candidates proclaim their programs. It was my lot, both in public school and Sunday school, when there was to be held a program, to declaim "Little Orphan Annie" or "The Raggedy Man."

In high school, four times I entered the oratorical contest, having the unenviable distinction of not placing at all in my freshman year, and being second the next three years, each time defeated by a different contestant. At Hobart College my only intercollegiate activity was serving on the debating team.

Since seminary days it has been my custom to listen to preaching on the radio and, whenever possible, to seek out notable preachers of whatever church that I might hear them. Under the direction of Dean Berryman Green I read widely in the field of sermons (actually written for the ear and not for the eye), but it was an interesting diet. As a chaplain in the United States Army, it was my privilege to hear many men of many faiths proclaim the Gospel to my edification.

When invited to give the George Craig Stewart Memorial Lectures on Preaching at the Seabury-Western Seminary, highly honored, I accepted, simply in the hope that through the experience of a very ordinary ministry as a parish priest, as Army chaplain, and as bishop of the church, I might with God's help speak simply and practically about this paramount function of the ministerial office, preaching.

In immediate preparation for the lectures some twenty-five or thirty books on the subject were read or reread—textbooks on homiletics, lectures on preaching, sermons themselves. This proved pure gain for me, the joy of rereading what had inspired and edified many years ago and the greater joy of discovery. In this survey I came to know for the first time Dr. Fuller's *What Is Liturgical Preaching?* and Dr. Dodd's *Apostolic Preaching,* both of which, in my opinion, should be required study for every clergyman in our church and for all preparing for ordination. These lectures abundantly testify my own indebtedness to these studies.

On the whole my reluctant and humbling conclusion was that after thirty years of preaching I had little technical knowledge of the subject. Many notes were taken and much was written. Discouraging was the realization that I was saying in different form and words what others had already said effectively.

With trash basket bulging, time escaping, and concern harassing an already distraught mind, I turned in real humility to the basic textbook for Christian preaching, the Scriptures. Reading therein it struck me that when St. Peter, in obedience to God's command, set forth to Cornelius the Christian Gospel, he went on to describe the apostolic ministry: "And he commanded us to preach unto the people, to testify that it is he which was ordained of God to be the Judge of quick and dead." (Acts 10:42)

From the text the phrase rang out, "Commanded to preach." It is imperative to consider this command in relation to our own ministries. We then seek to define and elucidate the who, why, what, and how of the art of preaching, that is, we seek answers to the questions, Who is commanded to preach? Why are we commanded to preach? What are we commanded to preach? and How are we commanded to preach?

I speak as a run-of-the-mill preacher, merely talking with you out of my own experience of preaching to hundreds of congregations in a myriad of circumstances—peace and war, at home and abroad, in cathedral and organized mission, on ship's deck and in an open field, to white and colored, to the naive and the sophisticated, the intellectual and the unlettered, the rich and the poor, perchance some saints and (God may judge) surely quite a few sinners.

My approach runs the risk of becoming preaching. Well, I am commanded to preach. It seems to me conceivable that it might be helpful for one whose primary ministry has been that of preaching to seek once again to define, describe, explain the high calling of the preacher, God's herald.

HENRY I. LOUTTIT

Contents

1

"Commanded to Preach"

IN A REPORT on the Athens Conference of the World Student Christian Federation, Finley Eversole relates this incident: "One morning Bishop Leslie Newbigin of the Church of South India, who delivered the biblical expositions each day, said, 'Stand up.' We stood. 'Sit down,' he said. We sat. 'I hope you get the point,' said Bishop Newbigin, 'words cause things to happen.'"[1]

The history of the immediate past supports this contention of Bishop Newbigin. Not least among the causes of World War II were the frenzied harangues of Adolf Hitler and the ceaseless and fervid speeches of Benito Mussolini. On the other hand, among the weapons which gave democracy the victory were the matchless oratory of Winston Churchill, and perhaps the fireside chats of Franklin Delano Roosevelt.

Commerce has no doubts about the value of the spoken word. The multimillion-dollar industries of radio and television have been built by advertising based on the principle that inane jingles constantly reiterated can sell goods. Our largest merchandisers and industrialists are not gullible and are not wasting tremendous amounts of time and money when they support this advertising.

But the truly important point is the abundant

testimony which scripture itself bears to the efficacy of the spoken word. The sacred writings consist largely, if not wholly, of reports of traditions long transmitted orally before having been committed to writing, or of materials written primarily to read aloud to a congregation.

Consider the Old Testament. The mighty act of creation is described in the book of Genesis in terms of speaking. "And God said, let there be . . . and there was." (1:13) God's relation to Israel constantly is symbolized as vocal utterance. "God spake all these words" (Exod. 20:1) introduces the proclamation of the Law. Isaiah bears witness to the common prophetic experience when he reports: "I heard the voice of the Lord." (6:8) "Because they obeyed not the voice of the Lord" (Josh. 5:6) is the reason given why the men of war who escaped from Egypt could not enter the promised land. Samuel's condemnation of Saul includes the charge: "Because thou hast not obeyed the voice of the Lord." (I Kings 20:36) Again and again Jeremiah declares: "This is a nation that obeyeth not the voice of the Lord their God." (7:28)

The importance of the spoken word in God's service is emphasized in the story of God's call to Moses. Moses, you recall, pleads his inability: "O my Lord, I am not eloquent, neither heretofore, nor since thou hast spoken unto thy servant: but I am slow of speech, and of a slow tongue." But God directs him thus: "Is not Aaron, the Levite, thy brother? I know that he can speak well. . . . And thou shalt speak unto him, and

18

put words in his mouth. . . . And he shall be thy spokesman unto the people." (Exod. 4:10–16)

This same reluctance and humility is reported of Jeremiah, "Then said I, Ah, Lord God! behold, I cannot speak for I am a child. . . . Then the Lord put forth his hand, and touched my mouth. And the Lord said unto me, Behold, I have put my words in thy mouth." (1:6–9) So, too, in the call of Ezekiel, "And he said unto me, Son of man, stand upon thy feet, and I will speak unto thee. . . . And thou shalt speak my words unto them, whether they will hear, or whether they will forbear." (2:1, 7) Following Isaiah's well-known response to the call of God, "Here am I; send me," the divine command is given, "Go, and tell this people." (6:8–9)

This same high valuation of the spoken word is also characteristic of the New Testament. No higher term or title for the eternal Son of God can be found than that given in the Prologue of St. John's gospel: "In the beginning was the Word, and the Word was with God, and the Word was God." (1:1) Here likewise is given the classical definition of the Incarnation: "The Word was made flesh, and dwelt among us, (and we beheld his glory, the glory as of the only begotten of the Father,) full of grace and truth." (1:14)

Often overlooked is the stern teaching of our Lord concerning words. "But I say unto you, That every idle word that men shall speak, they shall give account thereof in the day of judgment. For by thy words thou shalt be justified, and by thy words thou shalt be condemned." (Matt. 12:36–37) Our shock would be less if we remembered that two of the Ten Commandments, the basis of Israel's moral law, deal with speech—taking the name of the Lord in vain and bearing false witness against one's neighbor.

Although negative in its point of view, the Epistle of St. James bears forceful witness to the power of the human tongue and the necessity of its control: "If any man offend not in word, the same is a perfect man, and able also to bridle the whole body. . . . Even so the tongue is a little member, and boasteth great things. Behold, how great a matter a little fire kindleth! . . . Who is a wise man and endued with knowledge among you? Let him shew out of a good conversation his works with meekness of wisdom." (3:2–13)

The recognition of the significance, influence, and power of the living voice has characterized the Christian religion from its beginning. The story of the Christian faith begins, in a sense, with John the Baptist, last of the prophets, and forerunner of our Lord, whose primary work was preaching in order that men might be brought to repentance and baptism. "In those days came John the Baptist preaching in the wilderness of Judaea" (Matt. 3:1), "John bare witness of him, and cried, saying, This was he of whom I spake, he that cometh after me is preferred before me: for he was before me." (Jn. 1:15) "And many other things in his exhortation preached he unto the people." (Lk. 3:18)

Our Lord's own ministry was also primarily one of preaching. His mighty acts required words that men might know and understand their meaning. Following his baptism, and the arrest of John the Baptist, it is reported: "From that time Jesus began to preach, and to say . . ." (Matt. 4:17) "And he said unto them, Let us go into the next towns, that I may preach there also, for therefore came I forth." (Mk. 1:38) The word of Isaiah is his word in the synagogue at Nazareth where he had been brought up, "The Spirit of the Lord is upon me, because he hath anointed me to preach the gospel to the poor." (Isa. 61:1; Lk. 4:18) When the disciples of John the Baptist ask, "Art thou he that should come, or do we look for another?" he answers, "The poor have the gospel preached to them." (Matt. 11:3,5) Constantly we are told: "And he preached in their synagogues throughout all Galilee" (Mk. 1:39), "And he preached the word unto them" (Mk. 2:2), "On one of those days, as he taught the people in the temple, and preached the gospel." (Lk. 20:1)

It was his expectation that what he had begun would be continued in the church, the Body of Christ which becomes the extension of his incarnation. He speaks, "And this gospel of the kingdom shall be preached in all the world for a witness unto all nations." (Matt. 24:14) When the woman with the box of precious ointment is criticized for anointing him he prophesies, "Wheresoever this gospel shall be

21

preached in the whole world, there shall also this, that this woman hath done, be told for a memorial of her." (Matt. 26:13) St. Paul epitomizes our Lord's ministry: "But now in Christ Jesus ye who sometimes were afar off are made nigh by the blood of Christ. For he is our peace. . . . And came and preached peace to you which were afar off and to them that were nigh." (Eph. 2:13–14, 17)

Preaching, moreover, was always an important element in the work of the apostolic ministry. Certainly the early church understood the call and ordination of the Twelve to include the commission to preach. Hear St. Mark, "And he ordained twelve, that they might be with him, and that he might send them forth to preach." (3:14) And St. Matthew testifies: "These twelve Jesus sent forth, and commanded them, saying, Go not into the way of the Gentiles, and into any city of the Samaritans enter ye not: But go rather to the lost sheep of the house of Israel. And as ye go, preach, saying, the kingdom of heaven is at hand." (Matt. 10:5–7) Theirs is an expanding ministry. After our Lord's resurrection he appeared to the eleven and "said unto them, Go ye into all the world, and preach the gospel to every creature." (Mk. 16:15)

The story of the primitive church as related in both the gospels and the Acts of the Apostles is the story of preaching and its triumph. The Gospel according to St. Mark ends with the account of our Lord's ascension and the statement, "And they went forth and preached every where, the Lord working with them."

(16:20) That story continues in Acts beginning with St. Peter's great sermon on the Feast of Pentecost. "And daily in the temple, and in every house, they ceased not to teach and preach Jesus Christ." (Acts 5:42) In establishing a ministry of deacons, the Apostles plead, "It is not reason that we should leave the word of God, and serve tables." (6:2)

Persecution broadened the area of their preaching, "Therefore they that were scattered abroad went every where preaching the word." (Acts 8:4) This expanding ministry is exemplified by Philip: "passing through, he preached in all the cities, till he came to Caesarea." (Acts 8:40) It is their common task, "And they, when they had testified and preached the word of the Lord, returned to Jerusalem and preached the gospel in many villages of the Samaritans." (Acts 8:25)

What St. Peter declares to Cornelius concerning the ministry of the Apostles, "And he commanded us to preach unto the people" (Acts 10:42), St. Paul extols as his own calling, "For Christ sent me not to baptize, but to preach the gospel." (I Cor. 1:17) Paul is pre-eminently the preacher of the primitive church. He began immediately following his conversion, "Then was Saul certain days with the disciples which were at Damascus. And straightway he preached Christ in the synagogues, that he is the Son of God." (Acts 9:19-20) The formula of his whole missionary enterprise is that used to describe his early work with Barnabas: "They preached the word of God in the

23

synagogues of the Jews." (Acts 13:5) "And there they preached the gospel." (Acts 14:7)

St. Luke relates for us St. Paul's response to the vision of the man from Macedonia: "And after he had seen the vision, immediately we endeavoured to go into Macedonia, assuredly gathering that the Lord had called us for to preach the gospel unto them." (Acts 16:10) The final recorded word of St. Paul's ministry is in the prison house of Rome, "And Paul dwelt two whole years in his own hired house, and received all that came in unto him, preaching the kingdom of God and teaching those things which concern the Lord Jesus Christ." (Acts 28:30–31)

Paul's epistles abound with references to the supreme value of preaching. "It pleased God by the foolishness of preaching to save them that believe." (I Cor. 1:21) He writes to the church at Galatia, "it pleased God, who separated me from my mother's womb, and called me by his grace to reveal his Son in me, that I might preach him among the heathen." (1:15–16) To the church at Corinth he declares, "For though I preach the gospel, I have nothing to glory of: for necessity is laid upon me; yea, woe is unto me, if I preach not the gospel!" (I Cor. 9:16) For St. Paul the preaching of the Gospel is essential to man's salvation, "For whosoever shall call upon the name of the Lord shall be saved. How then shall they call on him in whom they have not believed? and how shall they believe in him of whom they have not heard? and how shall they hear without a preacher? And how shall they preach, except they be sent? as it is written, How beautiful are the feet of them that preach the gospel of peace, and bring glad tidings of good things!" (Rom. 10:13–15)

This same emphasis on preaching is found in the pastoral epistles. To Timothy it is written, "Whereunto I am ordained a preacher, and an apostle (I speak the truth in Christ, and lie not;) a teacher of the Gentiles in faith and verity." (I Tim. 2:7) The charge to Timothy is: "Preach the word; be instant in season, out of season; reprove, rebuke, exhort with all longsuffering and doctrine." (II Tim. 4:2) It is suggested: "Let the elders that rule well be counted worthy of double honour, especially they who labour in the word and doctrine." (I Tim. 5:17)

The Apostolic Church is ever mindful of the power of the spoken word of God: "For the word of God is quick, and powerful, and sharper than any twoedged sword, piercing even to the dividing asunder of soul and spirit, and of the joints and marrow, and is a discerner of the thoughts and intents of the heart." (Heb. 4:12)

The Acts of the Apostles is indeed the triumphant, victorious recital of the dramatic effectiveness of Christian preaching. When Paul and Silas came to Thessalonica, do you recall the charge which their Jewish adversaries made: "These [men] that have turned the world upside down are come hither also"? (Acts 17:6) The mighty works of God through his incarnate Son are translated into apostolic words that men may know salvation.

The mission of preaching continued, of course, after the close of the New Testament period. During the early centuries the Church hammered out its creed and its belief through preaching. Chrysostom, Athanasius, and Augustine immediately come to mind as great preachers. Without exception, every revival of the church's life, every surge of progress forward, was marked by fervent preaching. The Dark Ages ended, new life surged through the Church with the preaching of St. Francis, St. Dominic, St. Anselm, and St. Thomas Aquinas. Then came the Reformation and Luther's and Calvin's renewed emphasis on preaching the Word of God, with the result that the Christian Church—yes, the world—was changed. How powerfully preaching affects the world was further evidenced by the eighteenth-century evangelical revival, set on fire by the words of John Wesley and George Whitefield, and by the nineteenth-century revival, sparked by the sermons of John Newman and Edward Pusey.

The voices of those great stalwarts of the Christian pulpit had effect because they were seconded and echoed by preaching of less renown. In *The Shape of the Liturgy*, Dom Gregory Dix notes, when discussing the preaching of the later Middle Ages, an absence of doctrinal instruction in the homiletic literature of that period. This meant that the lay people went uninstructed and lacked any real understanding of the

Christian faith. Here was a weapon ready to hand that the Reformers were not slow to use. Dix points out, however, that in the homiletic literature of the period a steady note of moral instruction was sounded clearly and continually, an appeal to the emotions that the will might be moved to moral endeavor. With respect to the general collapse of morals in England during the reign of Edward VI (1547–53), which even the Reformers lamented, Dix argues that it must be attributed to the substitution of polemics for the earlier ethical preaching.

Accordingly, the prime importance of preaching in the primitive church as attested by scripture and our review of preaching as a chief function of the church historically, indicate the answer to the basic question, "Who are commanded to preach?" God calls his church in general, and his ministry in the church in particular, to preach his Word. Throughout the New Testament, by his words and actions, our Lord defines his ministry as having come forth to preach. A major part of Christ's earthly ministry was spent in teaching and training the Twelve whom he had chosen and ordained Apostles that they might be sent forth to preach in his name. In the great high priestly prayer he speaks, "As thou hast sent me into the world, even so have I also sent them into the world." (Jn. 17:18) As his continuing instrument of redemption, in order to continue his own ministry, he founds his church, i.e., he ordains and sends forth a ministry with the great commission, "Go ye therefore, and teach all nations, baptizing them in the name of the Father, and of the Son, and of the Holy Ghost: teaching them to observe all things whatsoever I have commanded you: and, lo, I am with you always, even unto the end of the world." (Matt. 28:19–20)

Both the book of Acts and the epistles testify that the Apostles conceived their ministry equally in terms of preaching and administering the sacraments. Everywhere exhortation and baptism go hand in hand; preaching is more mentioned than the laying on of hands; teaching and breaking bread with thanks is their ministry. This is the accepted understanding of the early church.

Dr. Fuller, in *What Is Liturgical Preaching?* points out: "For the authorized preacher of the word is the bishop (who was the preacher of the liturgical sermon in the early church, as well as the celebrant) or in his absence, the presbyter who is deputized for him. The ministry of the apostolic word and the dominical sacraments go together."[2] Fr. Paul Bull's *Preaching and Sermon Construction* quotes an Appendix by Bishop Gore to the "Report of the Archbishop's Commission on the Teaching Office of the Church": "The function of the minister is to preach the word of God, the message of salvation, as the apostles first delivered it. . . . The original idea of apostolic succession was centered upon the maintaining of the tradition."[3] In *The Shape of the Liturgy,* Dom Gregory Dix also reminds us that in the synaxis the sermon was the bishop's special liturgy as was the eucharistic prayer

28

in the offering of the Eucharist. From his throne behind the altar as representing God revealing himself to the world, the bishop speaks the authentic mind of the Church.[4]

Somehow in these latter days these two equal and essential functions of the ministry have become separated in our thinking. Catholic emphasis is upon the ministration of the sacraments. Protestant emphasis is upon the preaching of the Word. It is our thesis that these two primary functions of the ministry may not be separated without grave danger to the Christian Church and the Christian faith. At least this is the conviction of careful catholic scholarship. We quote three authorities—two Anglicans, one Roman.

Bishop Gore, for example, declares without qualification: "The chief function of the bishop and of any shepherd of souls is the preaching of the word of God."[5]

In his Introduction to *Preaching and Sermon Construction*, Fr. Bull sets forth the purpose of his effort: "I shall hope to show that it is a disaster to religion when the office of prophet and priest becomes detached, and as they found their proper union in the person of our Lord and Master, Jesus Christ, so it is our duty to him who entrusts us with his divine commission to try to fulfill faithfully both the prophetic and priestly aspect of our ministry."[6]

Liturgical Piety by Fr. Louis Bouyer speaks for Rome: "The whole significance, both of the apostolic ministry and of the Mystery of the Liturgy is gradually lost sight of when we separate the two offices of the priesthood—of preaching the word and performing the sacraments." And again, "The protestant reformers, especially Luther, were correct in their primary intuition of the fact that the word and the sacraments are never to be separated."[7]

This certainly is the implication of the Prayer Book rubric in the Order for the Administration of the Lord's Supper or Holy Communion, "Then followeth the Sermon. After which, the Priest, when there is a Communion, shall return to the Holy Table, and begin the Offertory. . . ." (p. 71)

Indeed, we can be even more specific in our answer to the question, "Who is commanded to preach?" We can reply: "We who are ordained bishops and priests in the church of God by that branch of the Anglican Communion known as the Protestant Episcopal Church in the United States of America." The Preface to the Ordinal indicates this clearly when it sets forth the intention of maintaining the orders of the ministry which have existed from the Apostles' time.

So important is the preaching function in the life of the church that it is limited strictly to those who have received episcopal ordination. Lay readers are not, save for urgent reasons, allowed the privilege and responsibility of preaching. The canon states: "He shall not deliver sermons or addresses of his own composition, unless, after instruction and examination, he be specially licensed thereto, for urgent reasons by the bishop."[8] Even deacons must be specially licensed by the bishop to preach the Gospel in the church of God. Among the proper collects for ordination only the collects for the consecration of a bishop specifically mention preaching: "Give grace, we beseech thee, to all Bishops, the Pastors of thy Church, that they may diligently preach thy Word" (BCP, p. 549); "so endue him with thy Holy Spirit, that he, preaching thy Word. . . ." (p. 559) The teaching is obvious. As in the early church, priests may preach only because they share in the episcopal and apostolic ministry by being deputized therefor. The privilege and responsibility are more vast because guarded so carefully.

In ordination to the priesthood the church's words are these: "so replenish them with the truth of thy Doctrine, and adorn them with innocency of life, that, both by word and good example, they may faithfully serve." (BCP, p. 537) This is the sentence following ordination: "Take thou Authority to preach the Word of God, and to minister the holy Sacraments in the Congregation where thou shalt be lawfully appointed thereunto." (p. 546) Finally we pray: "we beseech thee to send upon these thy servants thy heavenly blessing; that they may be clothed with righteousness, and that thy Word spoken by their mouths may have such success, that it may never be spoken in vain." (p. 547)

Partakers of the apostolic ministry are commanded to be preachers of the Word, as our ordination indicates. Remember we must that in the charge to the

31

deacon about to be ordered priest, the church speaks: "And if it shall happen that the same Church, or any Member thereof, do take any hurt or hindrance by reason of your negligence, ye know the greatness of the fault, and also the horrible punishment that will ensue." (BCP, 540) We dare not neglect the apostolic administration of the sacraments. We dare not neglect the apostolic ministry of preaching. To these are we called.

2

The Purpose
of Preaching

THE QUESTION which one who preaches must constantly ask himself is, Why am I saying this? What am I trying to accomplish? Indeed, some of the older generation of professors of homiletics advised that at the top of the first page of every sermon, before even the text was inscribed, there should be placed the statement, "The aim of this sermon is————." Purpose, then, is so important to Christian preaching, let us in this chapter consider it in some detail.

If normally we preached to homogeneous congregations—to repentant and forgiven sinners; to the converted who have personally accepted Jesus Christ as Lord and Saviour; to those desiring to grow in grace, seeking holiness, striving to increase in the knowledge of God as he has revealed himself in his incarnate Son; to followers of Christ committed to his service, trying earnestly to know and do his will—the problem of purpose would not be so complicated. Although even under that ideal condition, spiritual states and stages of sanctification would be so varied that some would need to be fed with milk and others with meat.

The average congregation is, in my opinion, so heterogeneous that it often seems that what the members have chiefly in common is their simultaneous presence at the service. I recall beginning an Easter sermon a good many years ago, with the question: Why are you here? My point was very simple. After reviewing the usual reasons the cynics give—namely, to display Easter finery (the vestigial remains of superstition) and to conform with social custom—I went on to point out that the overflowing congregation at Easter could not really be accounted for by these reasons. The cause of the annual miracle of worshiping multitudes must lie in some deep-seated, innate, overwhelming desire in them for something better and finer than ordinary life offers, of which the Resurrection is a promise.

How effective that sermon was remains unknown, but there were reactions. A day or two later a friend, at that time a nominal churchman, advised me that I had overlooked the chief reason for the attendance of the men—their wives had made them come! Nearly a year later, another man refused to make a pledge in the Every Member Canvass because he had been insulted. It seems that, although at great personal sacrifice he had come to the Easter service with his wife and child, the preacher ascended the pulpit, looked straight at him, and asked, "What are you doing here?" These two reactions may seem far-fetched, but on any Sunday morning the congregation, spiritually at least, is "of all sorts and conditions of men."

A good pastor knows this. He sees among his people: the man who has been, is, and fully intends to be unfaithful to his wife, but who is in church almost every Sunday; the leader of the church and community who truly believes that the communists have inspired people who say that Negroes should have equal rights as citizens and full acceptance as Christians; the pillar of the church who is insistent that the preacher stick to the Gospel, i.e., he should make no mention of economic, social, or political conditions or business or professional ethics unless, of course, the preacher more or less subtly offers support for cherished prejudices; the bride, here for the first time since her marriage, with her nominally Baptist husband and her militantly Baptist mother-in-law, who wants her pastor to make a good impression since mama-in-law has little patience with the Romish carryings-on of Episcopalians and as for people who pray from a book, "Well!"

There will also be present the "good" Mrs. Snipe who is so strongly against sin that she prates about it constantly—other people's sins, that is—to all who will give ear to listen. Mrs. Stalwart is always there; she is a leader of the women's work. Unfortunately her battle cry is, "There is so much to be done right here, why should we give our money to foreign missions?"

All of these and many others will be seated before the pastor; most of them, thank God, are at least trying to lead a better life. And some of them, praise God, have caught a vision, however beclouded, of his glory and seek to worship him. And the pastor trusts that his picture is not too cynical; certainly it is not bitter. All these he has loved and many more, for they are souls committed to his charge.

Yet each time he prepares to preach, the pastor confronts the nagging questions: Am I trying to bring to repentance those who need to repent? Am I seeking to convert the yet unconverted? Or should my effort be aimed at those on the way to sanctification? Should I be helping Christians become what they really are, to use the modern phrase? Is my purpose to set forth the saving faith in Jesus Christ our Lord? Or should my preaching define and elucidate that faith and its implications, moral, ethical, personal, social, political, and economic?

In addition to these questions, there is also sometimes the special problem of whom we are to address at the increasingly popular Family Service. This service started out to be one in which the whole parish family gathered in fellowship at the common board of the Supper of the Lord. Impossible in a congregation of appreciable size, it is a difficult service even when the church is large enough to accommodate all the communicants, because some members find it convenient to come early, others late; some desire music, others do not; one likes to listen to sermons and another avoids them like the plague. As a matter of fact, it has become that service which those with young children attend as a family unit. At this service the preacher faces the practical impossibility of talking at once to the first grader and the college graduate. The custom, as far as I have been able to observe, is to deliver a five-minute address aimed at the children and, after they leave, to instruct the adults. But this, Dr. Fuller quite rightfully points out, is not quite the same as preaching: "Teaching is not the direct and immediate aim of the sermon, properly understood. For the aim of the sermon is proclamation and response of faith."[1] And there is the question whether we who are "commanded to preach" dare ever merely teach or instruct our gathered people without adding the hortatory note which calls for a response of faith.[2]

In the Old Testament we hear little of formal preaching as such. The prophets spoke publicly, to be sure, but apparently on more or less isolated occasions and then to address the nation on moral, social, national, and international affairs and to bespeak God's judgment on Israel as a people, church, and nation. Jonah was sent specifically to preach to the Ninevites, and in this our Lord saw in him a sign, a forerunner of his own ministry, "For as Jonah was a sign unto the Ninevites, so shall also the Son of Man be to this generation." (Lk. 11:30)

Without doubt our Lord found the meaning and purpose of his own preaching in the "good tidings" of Second Isaiah (41:27), in the proclamation of the day of salvation. "The Spirit of the Lord God is upon me; because the Lord hath anointed me to preach good tidings unto the meek (Isa. 61:1), the gospel to the poor. . . . And he began to say unto them, This day is this scripture fulfilled in your ears." (Lk. 4:18, 21) The "good news" of the New Testament, then, is the announcement that the Messianic age has begun, the long awaited day of salvation is at hand, the acceptable year of the Lord (the era of God's favor) is dawning.

In the Gospel according to St. Mark, the account of Jesus' ministry begins: "Jesus came into Galilee, preaching the gospel of the kingdom of God, and saying, The time is fulfilled, and the kingdom of God is at hand: repent ye, and believe the gospel." (1:14–15) In this proclamation, Jesus strikes the eschatological note: the last days, the age of fulfillment are now in process of being realized. That all-inclusive phrase, "the kingdom of God," best summarizes our Lord's message. It has an apocalyptic element, but it has personal, social, and ethical elements also. We are most enlightened by our Lord's own commentary, "Thy kingdom come. Thy will be done." (Matt. 6:10) God's reign has begun in him. The sovereignty of God over the heart and mind and will of men makes explicit his eternal and universal sovereignty. In the words of Ernest F. Scott, "The Kingdom as he [Jesus] conceived it was at once the higher spiritual order, the better righteousness, the larger human brotherhood, the life of inward fellowship with God. None of these exclude the other."[3]

This proclamation of God's kingdom demands a response of repentance, faith, and obedience. Just as we all agree that the Douay translation of *metanoein*, "to do penance," is not adequate, so we must face the fact that repentance as regret and sorrow for sin falls far short of the full New Testament meaning of the word. Repentance has moral overtones, of course: a turning from sin to God, from evil to righteousness; but it means also a turning from error to truth, from ignorance to knowledge, from darkness to light, from death unto life. It is a call for a complete change in mind and heart and will. It is a call for reorientation to the new order, the new age, the new hope in God's revealed love; it is a call for a constant turning from the world with its temptations and its sins and for a re-turning toward the righteousness of God shown forth in Jesus Christ our Lord. It is the prodigal's return from the far country to his father's house. It is a gift of the Holy Spirit.

The awareness and acknowledgment of sin, upon which repentance is predicated, presents difficulties to the modern mind. Sociology with its stress on environment, genetics with its emphasis on heredity, and psychiatry with its insistence that the unconscious rules man, all conspire to clear the path of least resistance so that men need not face the fact of personal responsibility and guilt is merely an evil to be overcome. Hence, the need in preaching is to confront men with sin and God's judgment thereupon.

This does not mean that we should deal primarily with obvious and vulgar failures, confusing sins (which are symptoms) with sin (which is the disease). Men repent their sin, confess it, and strive by God's ⌣

41

grace to amend their lives only as they kneel in the presence of the Perfect One. Consequently, in our preaching, we seek primarily to confront men with God as he has revealed himself in Jesus Christ, Judge, and hence, Redeemer.

Only after Isaiah had caught the vision of God's glory in earth and heaven, was he able to say, "Woe is me! for I am undone; because I am a man of unclean lips, and I dwell in the midst of a people of unclean lips: for mine eyes have seen the King, the Lord of hosts." (6:5) Prostrate at Jesus' feet following the great draught of fishes, Simon Peter cried, "Depart from me; for I am a sinful man, O Lord." (Lk. 5:8) It is always in the clear white light of God's presence that the stains and shadows of our lives are clearly seen.

To believe the Gospel is to have faith. Such belief and faith is not merely intellectual assent to a proposition, a hypothesis, a doctrine, or a dogma. It is a response of utter trust in God's unfailing love proclaimed as the good tidings. It is Job's cry of anguish, "Though he slay me, yet will I trust in him." (13:15) It is our Lord's prayer in Gethsemane, "O my Father, if it be possible, let this cup pass from me: nevertheless not as I will, but as thou wilt." (Matt. 26:39) It is man's proper response to God's great love, to his proclaimed invitation to salvation; it is belief in, and acceptance with thanksgiving of, his proferred love.

To believe the Gospel is to be obedient to God's will as Christ's words in Gethsemane teach us. Alan

Richardson's point is well taken, though perhaps exaggerated: "In the New Testament generally, however, faith is closely associated with hearing, and in biblical language hearing is almost synonymous with obeying. The whole biblical theology is a theology of the word: God speaks his word, man must hear and obey . . . faith is response to the preached word of Christ, it is obedience to God's call to salvation."[4]

Certainly this our Lord demands, "Therefore whosoever heareth these sayings of mine, and doeth them, I will liken him unto a wise man, which has built his house upon a rock" (Matt. 7:24); and again, "Blessed are they that hear the word of God, and keep it" (Lk. 11:28). Like repentance, faith and obedience necessitate personal response, decision, and commitment; and yet they are gifts from God. God's action in Christ, Christ's proclamation of his eternal love, alone make such response possible. (The title of Reuel Howe's popular and much recommended study, *Man's Need and God's Action,* seemingly reverses the New Testament emphasis.) The aim, meaning, and purpose of our Lord's preaching, his proclaiming of God's kingdom, would seem to call for man's response of repentance, faith, and obedience to God's offer of salvation.

The response of obedience, even as of repentance and faith, eventuates in love. Thus our Lord summarizes the Law: "Thou shalt love the Lord thy God with all thy heart, and with all thy soul, and with all thy mind. This is the first and great commandment.

43

And the second is like unto it; Thou shalt love thy neighbour as thyself. On these two commandments hang all the law and the prophets." (Matt. 22:37–39)

So Jesus commands, "These things I command you, that ye love one another." (Jn. 15:17) In the Gospel according to St. John, the plea and the promise is this: "He that hath my commandments, and keepeth them, he it is that loveth me: and he that loveth me shall be loved of my Father, and I will love him, and I will manifest myself to him." (14:21) Of the woman with the alabaster box of ointment Jesus said, "Her sins, which are many, are forgiven; for she loved much: but to whom little is forgiven, the same loveth little." (Lk. 7:47) The faith of Simon Peter was revealed when to the question, "But whom say ye that I am?" he answered, "Thou art the Christ, the Son of the living God." (Matt. 16:15–16) Ultimately, to the threefold question, "Simon, son of Jonas, lovest thou me?" Simon Peter replies each time, "Thou knowest that I love thee." (Jn. 21:15–17)

St. Paul places this same emphasis on love also: "Though I speak with the tongues of men and of angels, and have not charity, I am become as sounding brass, or a tinkling cymbal. And though I have the gift of prophecy, and understand all mysteries, and all knowledge; and though I have all faith, so that I could remove mountains, and have not charity, I am nothing. And though I bestow all my goods to feed the poor, and though I give my body to be burned, and have not charity, it profiteth me nothing. . . . And now abideth faith, hope, charity, these three; but the greatest of these is charity." (I Cor. 13:1–3, 13) And the Johannine epistles declare: "Herein is love, not that we loved God, but that he loved us, and sent his Son to be the propitiation for our sins. Beloved, if God so loved us, we ought also to love one another" (I Jn. 4:10–11); and, "We love him, because he first loved us." (4:19)

The gospel record does distinguish between Christ's preaching and his teaching although they are closely allied. In St. Matthew it is written, "And Jesus went about all Galilee, teaching in their synagogues, and preaching the gospel of the kingdom." (4:23) His teaching is well exemplified in what we term the "Sermon on the Mount," which begins: "And seeing the multitudes, he went up into a mountain: and when he was set, his disciples came unto him: And he opened his mouth and taught them, saying. . . ." (Matt. 5:1–2) There then follows a discourse on the kind of righteousness which exceeds that of the scribes and Pharisees, and which is the ideal and goal of those who pray for and would inherit God's kingdom. Its end is: "that ye may be the children of your Father which is in heaven." (5:45)

This teaching demands a response of repentance, faith, and obedience, as does his teaching in parable, pronouncement, and miracle (the last, whatever else it may be, is dramatic teaching). The demand for response is less direct, less hortatory, less challenging, but it is not absent. He who proclaims salvation

45

teaches of God, of man, of himself as God-man, of men's relationship to God, and of men's relationship to each other. In so doing he describes the fruits of men's hearing the proclamation of the Gospel.

What he teaches, he commissions those who follow him to do. "He that receiveth you receiveth me, and he that receiveth me receiveth him that sent me" (Matt. 10:40), or more precisely, "He that heareth you heareth me" (Lk. 10:16). His assurance to the twelve and to the seventy as he sends them forth to preach the glad tidings is, "The kingdom of heaven is at hand" (Matt. 10:7).

It is to be noted that this preaching itself—his, theirs, that of the primitive church—is one of the signs of the arrival of the Age of Fulfillment. So also is it a necessary precondition of the completion of that age in the final things. When the disciples asked, "When shall these things be? and what shall be the sign of thy coming, and of the end of the world?" (Matt. 24:3), Jesus replied, "This gospel of the kingdom shall be preached in all the world for a witness unto all nations: and then shall the end come." (Matt. 24:14) And he made it clear that all this would take place in the midst of wars, persecution, and famine.

After his resurrection and immediately preceding his ascension, he gave to those called, trained, and ordained this commission: "Go ye into all the world, and preach the gospel to every creature." (Mk. 16:15) The good news of God's kingdom must be proclaimed to every man.

That the Apostles in particular and the primitive church in general accepted the commission and sought earnestly to obey, and thus to fulfill it, is evidenced by the whole New Testament. Indeed, what of necessity was only implicit in the pre-Passion proclamation of the Gospel could be made explicit from the post-Ascension vantage point.

As we suggested when we were speaking of our Lord's ministry, there is a clear distinction throughout the New Testament between preaching and teaching. New Testament preaching is specifically proclaiming the glad tidings of salvation to the non-Christian world. The Greek verb *keryssein* comes from *keryx* (herald), one who lifts up his voice to gain public attention to an important announcement. In New Testament usage "to proclaim" always has as its object, either expressed or implied, "the glad tidings." Hence, it becomes synonymous with *evangelizein,* to preach the good news.

New Testament teaching, on the other hand, is directed to those converted by the Gospel. In this ministry of the word, *paraklesis,* exhortation to renew and deepen the response of faith and obedience in the followers of the way, is distinguished from *didache,* instruction of the baptized in doctrine and in ethics, and, from, as Dr. Dodd notes, apologetics, the commending of the faith through reason to the interested but not yet converted.[5]

Whereas the Synoptic Gospels speak of preaching the good news or preaching the kingdom of God, in

47

both the book of Acts and the epistles, other terms are also used: preaching Jesus, preaching Christ, preaching the Word. Of the Samaritans it is said: "But when they believed Philip preaching the things concerning the kingdom of God, and the name of Jesus Christ, they were baptized, both men and women." (Acts 8:12)

The original apostolic ministry is described thus: "And daily in the temple, and in every house, they ceased not to teach and preach Jesus Christ." (Acts 5:42) And St. Paul, in the synagogue of the Jews in Thessalonica, for "three sabbath days reasoned with them out of the scriptures, opening and alleging, that Christ must needs have suffered, and risen again from the dead; and that this Jesus, whom I preach unto you, is Christ." (Acts 17:2–3)

The great missionary writes to the Romans of "the word of faith, of which we preach." (10:8) To the Corinthians, he writes, "We preach Christ crucified" (I Cor. 1:23), and "Woe is unto me, if I preach not the gospel!" (I Cor. 9:16) The admonition to Timothy is, "Preach the word: be instant in season, out of season." (II Tim. 4:2)

Whatever the descriptive terms used, the end and purpose of this preaching of the followers is the same as that of their Lord—to evoke the response of repentance, faith, obedience. On the day of Pentecost, following St. Peter's sermon, those who heard, "pricked in their hearts," cried out to the Apostles, "Men and brethren, what shall we do? Then Peter said unto them, Repent, and be baptized every one of you in the name of Jesus Christ for the remission of sins, and ye shall receive the gift of the Holy Ghost." (Acts 2:37–38)

The same note is sounded after the healing of the lame man at the Temple, "Repent ye therefore, and be converted." (Acts 3:19) Before the Sanhedrin, St. Peter speaks concerning Jesus, "And we are his witnesses of these things; and so is also the Holy Ghost, whom God hath given to them that obey him." (Acts 5:32) This proclaimed faith concerning Jesus Christ is summarized in these words: "Neither is there salvation in any other: for there is none other name under the heaven given among men, whereby we must be saved." (Acts 4:12)

St. Mark, we recall, opens his gospel with a proclamation: "The beginning of the gospel of Jesus Christ, the Son of God" (1:1); indeed, all the Synoptic Gospels are primarily expanded *kerygma,* the proclamation of glad tidings, the announcement of salvation, the Christian message of apostolic preaching. They contain, however, apostolic teaching also, both hortatory and instructive. St. Luke explains the purpose of his writing as "a declaration of those things which are most surely believed among us" (1:1); and in so doing, he sets forth the aim and purpose of all three: "that thou mightest know the certainty of these things, wherein thou hast been instructed." (1:4) Accordingly, throughout the Synoptic Gospels there is proclamation demanding a response of repentance, faith, and obedience, culminating in love. And the means par excellence to evoke this response of repentance, faith, obedience which culminates in love is the announcement that the Day of the Lord long foretold by the prophets has arrived; the proclamation of the advent of the Age to Come which is the burden of the apocalyptic message.

Our Lord begins his preaching ministry with the statement, "This day is this scripture fulfilled in your ears." (Lk. 4:21) Thus he interprets his power, "But if I cast out devils by the Spirit of God, then the kingdom of God is come unto you." (Matt. 12:28) On the way to Emmaus he chides Cleopas and his companion, "O fools, and slow of heart to believe all that the prophets have spoken. . . . And beginning at Moses and all the prophets, he expounded unto them in all the scriptures the things concerning himself." (Lk. 24:25,27) "The time is fulfilled, and the kingdom of God is at hand" (Mk. 1:15) is the theme of his preaching and the keynote of St. Mark and the other Synoptic Gospels. "This is that which was spoken by the prophet Joel; And it shall come to pass in the last days, saith God, I will pour out of my Spirit upon all flesh" (Acts 2:16–17) might well be called the "text" of St. Peter's sermon on Pentecost.

Our Lord proclaims the kingdom of God as the fulfillment of the promises of God in both prophetic and apocalyptic writings. His followers in turn proclaim him as King. This is the meaning of the triumphal entry into Jerusalem on that first Palm

Sunday harking back to the prophet Zechariah, "Behold, thy King cometh unto thee." (Zech. 9:9; Matt. 21:5) This is the truth set forth in the ironic superscription on the cross, "This is Jesus, the King of the Jews." (Matt. 27:37) And this is the insight of Revelation when the heavenly voices cry, "The kingdoms of this world have become the kingdoms of our Lord, and of his Christ; and he shall reign for ever and ever." (11:15)

In the Epistles of St. Paul written to and for the church, there is teaching, in the sense both of *didache* and *paraklesis,* rather than preaching in the sense of *kerygma;* but his teaching always presupposes and frequently refers to *kerygma.* For example, he sets forth his deepening understanding of the fulfillment of Christ thus: "when the fullness of time was come, God sent forth his Son. . . . that we might receive the adoption of sons. And because ye are sons, God hath sent forth the Spirit of his Son into your hearts, crying Abba, Father." (Gal. 4:4–6) The pouring out of the Holy Spirit is the sign of the Age to Come, and reference to it is constantly made in the New Testament. This Age, which was seen first in mighty signs and wonders and in unusual psychical phenomena, now is seen as a consummation which bestows a new quality of life, individual and social, befitting those redeemed and adopted as sons. The fruits of the Spirit in Galatians (5:22–23), the gifts of the Spirit in I Corinthians (12), find their zenith in *agape,* and they characterize the new creature who is "in Christ" even

51

as "the fellowship of the spirit" characterizes the new order of the Age to Come, which is the Church, the Messianic community, the Israel of God, the Body of Christ.

Accordingly, the supernatural order of life, long foretold in somewhat naive terms, is now present, as an actual fact of human experience, in Christ's church, which is the earnest and assurance of life's final consummation in his heavenly kingdom when he comes again. This is realized eschatology in its fullness. This also spells out the final meaning of the response—in repentance, faith and obedience, the apogee of which is love—to the proclamation of the *kerygma*, which in the Pauline formula is the simple statement, "Jesus is the Lord." (I Cor. 12:3)

The Gospel according to St. John is, like the Synoptic Gospels, a true gospel—that is, *kerygma* interpreted. But the eschatology which forms the basis of New Testament proclamation becomes sublimated in St. John's gospel. The kingdom of God becomes "eternal life": "And this is life eternal, that they might know thee the only true God, and Jesus Christ whom thou hast sent." (17:3) Like the epistles of St. Paul, the Gospel according to St. John epitomizes the *kerygma* in proclaiming the incarnate Son, though St. John prefers as his title "the Word," rather than St. Paul's title, "Lord." John's text, throughout his gospel, is: "The Word was made flesh, and dwelt among us (and we beheld his glory, the glory as of the only begotten of the Father) full of grace and truth." (1:14)

This résumé of the end and purpose of the preaching, and for that matter of the teaching, in the New Testament, should serve to underline the fact that like St. Paul we are commanded to preach, "not ourselves, but Christ Jesus the Lord." (II Cor. 4:5) To preach "Jesus Christ, and him crucified" (I Cor. 2:2) is not merely to seek intellectual acceptance of certain truths, to move the will to high moral endeavor, to induce an emotional response of either yearning or enthusiasm; it is to confront man with God as he has revealed himself in the mighty act of redemption through his incarnate Son. The purpose of such preaching now, as in the primitive church, is to win men's response in repentance, faith, and obedience, to bring men to love that they may be brought to Love.

In his classic lectures, *On Preaching*, Phillips Brooks defines preaching as "the communication of truth by man to men. . . . the bringing of truth through personality." Here the word *Truth* should be capitalized, for he further counsels, "Beware of the tendency to preach about Christianity, and try to preach Christ." His answer to our question, "What is preaching for?" is simply, "It is for men's salvation."[6]

With this Fr. Bull agrees, but he goes on to point out that preaching has a corporate as well as an individualistic aim, and that both are necessary. Merely to preach for the sake of conversion and that men's souls be saved may well end in a spiritual selfishness, not to say smugness; whereas merely to preach submission to the Church may well result in complacent conformity rather than holiness.[7]

This dual emphasis is shown in our Lord's proclaiming the kingdom of God on the one hand, and his calling for repentance and faith on the other. This corporate aspect of preaching is, of course, also an emphasis of Dr. Fuller in his study of liturgical preaching: "The purpose of the liturgical sermon is to renew in the individual members the sense that they are members of the *ecclesia,* constituted as such by the redemptive act of God in Christ."[8]

Thus, the end of our preaching must be "so to present Jesus Christ in the power of the Holy Spirit, that men may be won to put their trust in God through him, to accept him as their Saviour, and to serve him as their King in the fellowship of his church."[9] As part of the long succession of those "commanded to preach," we too must seek to bring men to a personal encounter with God in Christ, to the response of repentance, faith, obedience, and to that love which is the keynote of Christian life both individual and corporate.

While we grant the kerygmatic character of preaching in the primitive church, and agree that liturgical preaching should include what in the New Testament is classified as *paraklesis,* we maintain that preaching must also include *didache,* instruction in doctrine and morals.

We would insist upon this for three reasons: First, the situation in which we find ourselves today is not unlike the one faced by the early church. In fact, we too are preaching weekly to nonbelievers, to religiously illiterate believers, and to repentant and forgiven believers who seek the grace to grow in sanctity.

Second, most of us preach to congregations which do not center their devotion and their life in the Eucharist.

And third, we are speaking, for the most part, to people who are grossly ignorant not only of theology—moral, ascetic, and dogmatic—but of the Bible and the basic tenets of the Christian faith.

In actual practice, the pulpit at the public services offers the one opportunity the priest has to edify and to instruct, to challenge and to renew, the majority of the souls committed to his charge. All this cannot be done in every sermon, but it is the program to be carried out sooner or later in our preaching. Moreover, I am personally convinced that every time we address our gathered people, be it at the meetings of organizations, at classes of instruction for inquirers, adults, or children, the note of preaching must not be absent. Always we should be seeking to bring men face to face with God in Christ, demanding that response of repentance, faith, obedience, that response of love which is salvation.

We too must proclaim the Gospel to a nonbelieving and a disbelieving world. We preach not so much to those who have never heard, but to those who hear yet heed not. We must make the sermon, particularly at the Eucharist (to use the words of Dr. Fuller), "a bridge between Baptism and the Eucharist." Dr. Barth has also observed, "Baptism and the Lord's Supper form what we may call the natural bounds of the church service."[10]

Our purpose, then, is "to extract from the scripture readings the essential core and content of the gospel, to penetrate beyond the day's pericope to the proclamation of the central act of God in Christ, which it contains, in order that the central act of God can be made the material for recital in the prayer of Thanksgiving."[11] The service of the Word, including the sermon, is a recalling of the saving acts of God in Jesus Christ before the congregation: "But this recalling before man is the preliminary to the recalling of the events before God by way of eucharistic recital, so that God in turn may make these events actually present to the participants."[12]

If church people on the whole are not eucharistically minded and if their practice of religion is not centered on the Supper of the Lord, it may well be because we who preach have failed to make the sermon the connecting link between the service of the Word and the service of Thanksgiving. Fr. Bouyer reminds us of the close interrelation in the Christian liturgy between speaking and doing, between pulpit and altar, for the liturgy centers in the action of the Word. We quote: "The Liturgy in its unity and in its perfection is to be seen as the meeting of God's people called together in convocation by God's Word through the apostolic ministry, in order that the people, consciously united together, may hear God's Word itself in Christ, may adhere to that Word by means of prayer and praise amid which the Word is proclaimed, and so seal by the Eucharistic sacrifice the Covenant which is accomplished by that same Word."[13]

Perhaps it is not too strong to say that in one sense at least the aim of this central act of Christian worship and the end of Christian preaching is the same, to win that response of repentance, faith, obedience, culminating in love which characterizes God's people. Certainly, it is significant that in the Order for the Holy Communion this demand is set forth in the invitation, "Ye who do truly and earnestly repent you of your sins, and are in love and charity with your neighbours, and intend to lead a new life, following the commandments of God, and walking from henceforth in his holy ways; Draw near with faith, and take this holy Sacrament to your comfort; and make your humble confession to Almighty God, devoutly kneeling." (BCP, p. 75)

That this response is inextricably bound up with the Eucharist is the teaching of the church in the Office of Instruction. To the question, "What is required of those who come to the Lord's Supper?" the answer is given: "to examine themselves, whether they repent them truly of their former sins, with stedfast purpose to lead a new life; to have a lively faith in God's mercy through Christ, with a thankful remembrance of his death; and to be in charity with all men." (BCP, p. 293)

But there must be another goal in our preaching, one which the Ordinal reiterates so that it tolls like a bell throughout the service—namely, that the church may be edified. Hence, teaching, *didache,* must find place in any consideration of preaching. By this we mean not merely the calling attention to facts, the securing of intellectual assent to truths, or the imparting of the knowledge of God which our Lord defines as eternal life. Fr. Voillaume once wrote to the Little Brothers of Jesus: "The church is a body living by a life whose mystery is something beyond us all. Its growth is no less one of depth in souls than of outward extension in numbers. It may well be, in fact, that the greater of the two dimensions is not its breadth but its depth. In this latter dimension, the church defies all measurement, lends itself to no statistics, however highly developed."[14]

Accordingly, to us who are commanded to preach the directive is given, as it was to the Ephesians: "And he gave some, apostles; and some, prophets; and some, evangelists; and some, pastors and teachers; For the perfecting of the saints, for the work of the ministry, for the edifying of the body of Christ: Till we all come in the unity of the faith, and of the knowledge of the Son of God, unto a perfect man, unto the measure of the stature of the fulness of Christ." (4:11–13)

3

The Content of Preaching

"WHAT SHALL I preach about next Sunday?" is the Monday morning question which confronts most pastors. The pressure of this demanding, nagging, and immediate question will be lessened appreciably if the pastor tries to answer once and for all the fundamental question, What am I commanded to preach? What shall be the content of my preaching? Or more precisely, *who* is the subject of my proclamation?

To keep in mind the *who* of that final question is to be saved from the more flagrant and less excusable errors in preaching. With St. Paul we must have it burned into our memory: "We preach not ourselves but Christ Jesus the Lord; and ourselves your servants for Jesus' sake." (11 Cor. 4:5) No man wittingly would damn his soul by putting "I" in place of Christ in pulpit utterance but unhappily the dereliction is not unknown, though unconscious.

Far too many preachers make of themselves news commentators with a religious bias. Sunday by Sunday, such preachers render their weighty judgments on the passing scene—as reported in *Time, Newsweek,* and the daily press, forgetting that most of their hearers are literate also. How many sermons originated in the *Reader's Digest* before that publication became so widely read that the source of inspiration was obvious!

A preacher is really wasting precious pulpit time when he sets forth his own ideas on any subject, including the Christian religion. He misuses an opportunity, which the church provides in the public service at sermon time, when he scolds or when he defends his own position, statements, or actions. Someone has designated "I" the most indecent of the pronouns. Avoid it as a plague in preaching. I want, I believe, I think, may be of real interest to the speaker; they could not matter less to souls that need salvation. In reality they betray a pride that leadeth to damnation.

When Christ is the center of our life, our thought, and our preaching, we are also saved from other more understandable yet widespread errors. One of these is to make the sermon a lecture in dogmatic theology, introduced by the phrase, "the church teaches," or with sticky sentimentality, "Mother Church tells us." Propositional theology, even sound argument appealing to the reason, also misses the mark. Sam Shoemaker, one of the great preachers of the Episcopal Church, frequently quoted this observation of Lord Lindsay, one time Master of Balliol College, Oxford: "You ministers are making a mistake. In your pulpits you're arguing for Christianity. And no one wants arguments. You ought to be witnessing. Does this thing work? Then share it with the rest of us."[1]

To agree with Lord Lindsay is not to imply that

doctrine has no place in the pulpit; it is to emphasize that the goal of preaching is not to make the members of the congregation learned in theology but to bring them to complete commitment. Phillips Brooks has well expressed this goal: "Preach doctrine, preach all the doctrine that you know and learn forever more and more; but preach it always, not that men may believe it, but that men may be saved by believing it."[2]

Another widespread error is to make the sermon a mere moral homily. We rejoice that the "be good and you'll be happy" school is passing from the scene. But there remain other and not too dissimilar misunderstandings about the Christian faith. The "peace of mind" cult prostitutes the Gospel when it panders to men's selfish pursuit of happiness (not to say health, success, and prosperity) and is blind to the fact that the Christian ideal is the imitation of Christ, not the pursuit of happiness.

At the opposite extreme are the "thou shalt not" brethren, the heirs of the Puritan tradition, who thunder denunciations from their pulpits, equating pleasure with sin and making joy a crime. To make this emphasis is to forget that "the law was given by Moses, but grace and truth came by Jesus Christ." (Jn. 1:17)

In any case, to limit preaching to a presentation of Christian ethics, Christian conduct, or even Christian moral theology is to make of a part, the whole. For Christian morals, ethics, and conduct are the fruits of the Christian's new relationship to God in Christ and spring out of it. Christ is the content of our preaching. Only in encounter with him are life and one's way of living changed.

Less usual, though not unknown in our church, yet heard constantly in the so-called "gospel preaching" on the radio and among sectarians is preaching of the kind that appeals mainly to the emotions. The better word to describe this preaching is perhaps "enthusiastic" (in the basic sense of that misused term) but that might be too devastating a judgment! In the Episcopal Church the more grievous fault is to turn the Gospel into a placebo aimed at making our people feel good inside, awakening a warm glow of pleasure in their hearts. Witness the saccharine Christmas sermons of the "Babe in the manger" type, the too frequent confusion of *agape* with romantic love, and the sentimentalities issuing forth on Mother's Day. Emotion is vital in religion, but it is a means, not an end. Subject matter that is chosen primarily to arouse emotions offers the starving candy in place of wholesome bread.

The obvious implication of our discussion thus far is that the content of our preaching will be dependent on its purpose and its aim. As heirs of the apostolic tradition, preachers will do well in this matter, as in others, to search the scriptures.

In preaching, as in all else, we seek to follow him whom we call Lord and Master. What, then, was the content of his message? Our Lord's ministry began and ended with scripture; scripture formed the basis of his preaching. In the synagogue at Nazareth he defined his ministry on the basis of the sixty-first chapter of Isaiah. On the cross his cry was from Psalm 22, "My God, my God, why hast thou forsaken me?" (Ps. 22:1; Matt. 27:45), the psalm which ends on the note of victory, "For the kingdom is the Lord's: and he is the governor among the nations." (Ps. 22:28) The words of the voice from heaven at his baptism are more than reminiscent of the Messianic Psalm 2, "Thou art my Son; this day have I begotten thee." (Ps. 2:7) The Suffering Servant of Second Isaiah defines his passion and indeed his understanding of Messiahship: "He is despised and rejected of men; a man of sorrows, and acquainted with grief: . . . . Surely he hath borne our griefs and carried our sorrows. . . . he was wounded for our transgressions, he was bruised for our iniquities . . . with his stripes we are healed." (Isa. 53:3–5) To this he referred as he came down from the Mount of Transfiguration and set his face toward Jerusalem: "it is written of the Son of man, that he must suffer many things, and be set at nought." (Mk. 9:12) In the Upper Room as the hour of betrayal approached he declared: "For I say unto you, that this that is written must yet be accomplished in me, and he was reckoned among the transgressors." (Lk. 22:37)

To the scripture our Lord constantly referred. Concerning the stone which the builders rejected, he asked, "Did ye never read in the scriptures?" (Matt. 21:42) To the Sadducees who would argue there is no resurrection he replied, "Ye do err, not knowing the scriptures." (Matt. 22:29) In the case of Cleopas and his companion it is reported, "And beginning at Moses and all the prophets, he expounded unto them in all the scriptures the things concerning himself." (Lk. 24:27)

From the Old Testament came the content of his preaching. The kingdom of God, the dominant theme of his message, is not an Old Testament phrase, but it expresses a constant Old Testament concept. "His kingdom is an everlasting kingdom, and his dominion is from generation to generation," Daniel proclaims. (4:3) And the psalmist declares, "The Lord hath prepared his throne in the heavens; and his kingdom ruleth over all." (Ps. 103:19) The vision of Obadiah, "the kingdom shall be the Lord's" (v. 21), is the insight of all the prophets.

Central to Jesus' thought were other Old Testament concepts. The God who reigns as king is also God the Father of his people and the Good Shepherd of his flock. Sings the psalmist, "A father of the fatherless, and a judge of the widows, is God in his holy habitation." (Ps. 68:5) And the promise of Jeremiah concerning the restoration of Israel was: "I am a father to Israel and Ephraim is my firstborn." (31:9) To countless generations have these words brought hope: "The Lord is my shepherd; I shall not want." (Ps. 23:1) Isaiah depicts the day of the Lord, "He shall feed his flock like a shepherd: he shall gather the lambs with his arm, and carry them in his bosom, and shall gently lead those that are with young." (40:11)

His chosen Messianic title is from Daniel's vision, "the Son of man." (7:13) In his summary of the Law that characterizes those who accept God's rule, he combines Deuteronomy 6:5 with Leviticus 19:18, "Thou shalt love the Lord thy God with all thine heart, and with all thy soul, and with all thy might— thou shalt love thy neighbour as thyself." To all of these ancient concepts, of course, he brings new insights, new understanding, new interpretation; he enriches them with fuller content.

The prophet out of Nazareth was indeed at one with the ancient prophets when they cried: "Thus saith God the Lord." (Isa. 42:5) This is the testimony of St. Matthew: "The people were astonished at his doctrine: for he taught them as one having authority, and not as the scribes." (7:28–29) St. John's later understanding is even more explicit: "My doctrine is not mine, but his that sent me. If any man will do his will, he shall know of the doctrine, whether it be of God, or whether I speak of myself." (7:16–17)

Note well the content of Christ's message, and how he sets it forth. He persuades not with argument but with affirmation (witness the Sermon on the Mount); he convinces by simple story and telling parable, not by striking syllogism or bald theological proposition. He deals not with the abstract but with the concrete, not with the attributes of God but with the good God who is our Father; not with love as a philosophical concept, but with the attitudes of the father of the prodigal, the Good Samaritan, the woman with the alabaster box of ointment; not with virtues but the trustful centurion, "I say unto you, I have not found so great faith, no, not in Israel" (Lk. 7:9), with one who "was sad at that saying, and went away grieved: for he had great possessions" (Mk. 10:22), with "the unjust steward." (Lk. 16:8) In parable, metaphor, simile, he speaks simply of God, of man, of men's relationship to God and to other men, of his own place in the grand economy of God, of his relationship to God the Father, to those called and chosen, to the world of men.

These same themes and emphases mark apostolic preaching as the New Testament testifies. In the light of the Resurrection and in the fulfilled promise of the gift of the Holy Spirit, Christ becomes the content of apostolic preaching. Primary emphasis is not on what he said, but on what he did—yes, on who he was and is. Their proclamation of the glad tidings of God's proferred salvation is summed up in the *kerygma*.

C. H. Dodd, in his valuable study, analyzes the kerygmatic element in the sermons reported in the Acts of the Apostles. He shows it to be in reality an expansion of the summary of our Lord's preaching given by St. Mark: "Jesus came into Galilee preaching the gospel of the kingdom of God, and saying, The time is fulfilled, and the kingdom of God is at hand: repent ye, and believe the gospel." (1:14–15) The same proclamation or *kerygma* is stated, he notes, although not so concisely, in St. Paul's epistles, forms the backbone of the fourfold gospel, and later received summary statement in the creeds of the church.

The proclamation, then, of the primitive church included the following elements: First, it proclaims that the time of fulfillment foretold by the prophets is here through the ministry, death, and resurrection of Christ, the seed of David, who is now exalted on the right hand of God and whose present power is evidenced by the Holy Spirit in the church (shown forth, be it said in passing, in part at least by the church's preaching). Then, it states the assurance that the Messianic age will soon reach its consummation in Christ, who is the Son of God and Lord, and who as Saviour is the judge of the quick and the dead. In conclusion, it appeals for repentance and offers the promise of forgiveness.[3]

In describing what the preachers of the primitive church proclaimed, Dr. Dodd indicates what the preacher must do in our age and time: "The great thinkers of the New Testament period, while they worked out bold, even daring ways of restating the original gospel, were so possessed by its fundamental convictions that their restatements are true to its first intention. Under all variations of form, they continue to affirm that in the events out of which the Christian Church arose there was the conclusive act of God, who in them visited and redeemed his people, and that in the corporate experience of the church itself there was revealed a new quality of life, arising out of what God had done, which in turn corroborated the value set upon the facts."[4]

It is true, of course, as suggested earlier, that, with the passage of time, the vocabulary changed. Whereas our Lord preached the kingdom of God and talked of the Son of man, St. Paul spoke of the Body of Christ and proclaimed that Jesus Christ is Lord. St. John understood these concepts as eternal life and the Word made flesh who dwelt among us.

Mark well that the *kerygma* begins with the scriptures. How very difficult, not to say impossible, is it to understand the New Testament save on the basis of the older writings. St. Peter began his sermon on the experience of Pentecost: "But this is that which was spoken by the prophet Joel; And it shall come to pass in the last days, saith God, I will pour out of my Spirit upon all flesh: and your sons and your daughters shall prophesy, and your young men shall see visions, and your old men shall dream dreams." (Acts 2:16–17) The Gospel according to St. Mark opens: "The beginning of the gospel of Jesus Christ, the Son of God; as it is written in the prophets, Behold, I send my messenger before thy face, which shall prepare thy way before thee." (1:1–2) In the synagogue at Antioch in Pisidia, St. Paul started his missionary enterprise and preaching, "The God of this people of Israel chose our fathers." (Acts 13:17) Reviewing history he interpreted Israel's rejection of his Lord, "For they that dwell at Jerusalem, and their rulers, because they knew him not, nor yet the voice of the prophets which are read every sabbath day, they have fulfilled them in condemning him." (Acts 13:27)

They, too, recognized that it is God who speaks through them. The Acts of the Apostles in describing St. Peter before the Sanhedrin set forth the primitive Christian belief, "Then Peter, filled with the Holy Ghost, said unto them." (4:8) St. Paul writes to the church at Ephesus concerning his ministry: "Whereof I was made a minister, according to the gift of the grace of God given unto me by the effectual working of his power. Unto me, who am less than the least of all saints, is this grace given, that I should preach among the Gentiles the unsearchable riches of Christ." (3:7–8) The author of the Epistle to the Hebrews sums up the Christian understanding in these words: "God, who at sundry times and in divers manners spake in time past unto the fathers by the prophets, hath in these last days spoken unto us by his Son." (1:1–2) In speaking of marriage to the Corinthians, St. Paul clearly distinguishes between what he thinks and what is given him to say, "But I speak this by permission, and not of commandment." (I Cor. 7:6)

In addition to the *kerygma* proclaiming the way of salvation to the unconverted, there is to be distinguished in the New Testament, Dr. Fuller points out, at least two other types of the ministry of the Word. The first is *paraklesis,* "the renewal and deepening of the *kerygma* in the already converted," that is, the exposition of the ethical and doctrinal implications of the *kerygma,* with exhortation to follow steadfastly in the Way.[5] This is seen clearly in the epistles. Again and again St. Paul sounds this note one way or another: "I beseech you therefore, brethren, by the mercies of God, that ye present your bodies a living sacrifice, holy, acceptable unto God, which is your reasonable service. And be not conformed to this world; but be ye transformed by the renewing of your mind, that ye may prove what is that good, and acceptable, and perfect, will of God." (Rom. 12:1–2) The other type is *didache* (instruction), the teaching of ethics and doctrine. This may well be the meat to which St. Paul refers when he tells the Corinthians, "I have fed you with milk, and not with meat: for hitherto ye were not able to bear it, neither yet now are ye able." (I Cor. 3:2) All three—*kerygma, paraklesis,* and *didache*—are to be found throughout the New Testament and all three must be considered in our preaching.

In accordance with the Constitution of the Protestant Episcopal Church in the United States of America, no man is ordained to any order of the sacred ministry in the church of God unless and until he shall subscribe and make the following declaration in the presence of the ordaining bishop or bishops: "I do believe the holy Scripture of the Old and New Testament to be the word of God, and to contain all things necessary to salvation; and I do solemnly engage to conform to the doctrine, discipline, and worship of the Protestant Episcopal Church in the United States of America."[6]

Since the end of preaching is the salvation of men —winning that response of repentance, faith, obedience, which culminate in love of God and men; seeking conversion, commitment, sanctification of the souls committed to our charge—it follows that our preaching must be scriptural; that is to say, it must be based on and in accordance with the "things necessary to salvation" found in the scriptures.

I would not argue that it is absolutely essential to use a text but would insist that the use of a text is a safeguard to hold pastors to their pledged trust and responsibility. Then too, it is of great practical value. If the members of the congregation forget what the preacher says and remember the text, they will have gained much. I would not argue that sermons be replete with scriptural quotations, though frequently the truth is stated there far better than the preacher can say it. I would insist that the whole sermon conform to the faith the scripture plainly teaches.

Toward this end, the renewed interest in and understanding of biblical theology in our day—for many valuable studies are being published in that field—is a great boon to us who are called upon to preach the word of God that the Word may be revealed. This is to say, we are called to "preach not ourselves, but Christ Jesus the Lord." (II Cor. 4:5) The content of our preaching, then, is the eternal God as he has re-

vealed himself in Jesus Christ our Lord and through
the Holy Spirit all plainly set forth in scripture. The
content of a given sermon will vary, of course, with
its aim and purpose, but our preaching must include
the three types of the ministry of the Word found in
the church of the New Testament. Not only is there
a place for the *kerygma* in the Episcopal Church today; it is our greatest single need. We tend too much
to envision preaching as God speaking through his
servant to his gathered people, and far too little in
seeing it as God speaking through his church to a
damned and dying world. Proclaiming the Good
News to unsaved and unconverted men is essential if
we are to be obedient to our Lord's express command and to fulfill the mission of the church. But
when and how—living as most of us will in a Christian nation and dealing for the most part with profes-
sing Christians?

We must face realistically the fact that nearly 50
per cent of the population of these United States
does not claim membership in any religious body
and, for a large share of those who do claim such
allegiance, their membership is a nominal matter for
purposes of convenience only. In every public speaking engagement, regardless of the program or the subject of our address, we can say at least a word of
witness for our Lord. In brief, we can preach Christ.

In this day and time all of us, at one time or another, will be given the privilege of speaking over the
local radio (usually through the good offices of the

local ministerial association to which we should belong). What better opportunity is there to proclaim the Christian faith?

There is a real need and place for this type of preaching to our own congregations also. In every organization in the congregation, there are the uncommitted and the unconverted folk. Time and time again we have opportunity to speak to them. On occasion, preaching for conversion and commitment has a place in the regular services of the church. There will be those present who need it. A word of caution is in order, however. Nothing is more trying, not to say boring, to those in the pew than to hear the one note, "You must be converted now," sounded from the pulpit Sunday after Sunday.

The great opportunity, in our opinion, for kerygmatic preaching, is with confirmation classes. Sacraments are not magic. God has created men in his own image, which is to say that he has shared with us the ability to feel and think and will. He has shared with us his freedom. To be saved necessitates response, decision, the acceptance of God's freely offered gift. The grace given in the initiatory rite, the sacraments of baptism and confirmation, the gifts of the Holy Spirit received therein aid men to respond properly to the Gospel.

The proclamation of the faith, the *kerygma*, aims at evoking that response of repentance, faith, obedience, love that makes possible a "daily increase in

[his] Holy Spirit more and more, until [we] come into [his] everlasting kingdom." (BCP, p. 297)

It is interesting to know, of course, that Henry VIII did not found the Anglican Communion; to have penetrated the mystery of the J.E.D.P. sources of the Pentateuch; to learn that one normally genuflects in reverence to our Lord when the sacrament is reserved; and even to understand the Sulpician method of mental prayer; but these are hardly necessary for salvation. Why deal with nonessentials with a group of people preparing to accept full adult privilege and responsibility as church members?

Over these candidates, the church will pray, "Almighty and everliving God, who hast vouchsafed to regenerate these thy servants by Water and the Holy Ghost, and hast given unto them forgiveness of all their sins." (BCP, p. 297) Surely we must make certain they understand regeneration: that, in the initiatory rite by the power of God, we who are incorporated into Christ's mystical body literally die to sin and the world, are buried with Christ in his death, and are raised with him into this new kind of life which we call Christian. Must we not hope and pray that, through the guidance of the Holy Spirit, this death and resurrection experience will be made real to them? With St. Paul we must proclaim to them, "Know ye not, that so many of us as were baptized into Jesus Christ were baptized into his death? Therefore we are buried with him by baptism into death: that like as Christ was raised up from the dead by the glory of the Father, even so we also should walk in newness of life." (Rom. 6:3–4)

These are they who, we dare to hope, will present themselves at least weekly before the altar of God. They will join with the eternal priest as he reiterates that Christ made "(by his one oblation of himself once offered) a full, perfect, and sufficient sacrifice, oblation, and satisfaction, for the sins of the whole world" (BCP, p. 80). At one with God, they will offer and present unto him themselves, their "souls and bodies, to be a reasonable, holy, and living sacrifice." (BCP, p. 81)

In the confirmation service, the bishop asks, "Do you promise to follow Jesus Christ as your Lord and Saviour?" Why not make our aim to insure that the "I do" response is not merely ritualistic but represents conversion and commitment? We must ever keep before us and our people the insight of John Donne's famous statement, "I shall not live till I see God; and when I have seen him I shall never die." Is not this the ultimate meaning of the prayer, "Let thy fatherly hand, we beseech thee, ever be over them; let thy Holy Spirit ever be with them; and so lead them in the knowledge and obedience of thy Word, that in the end they may obtain everlasting life." (BCP, p. 298)

The content of the *kerygma* in our modern preaching remains, of course, what it has always been— Christ, the incarnate Son of God, Redeemer, Lord, and King. We proclaim before men the mighty acts of God, culminating in the event, God coming to dwell with men in the person of his Son, marking the inaugurating of the new age.

Preaching the *kerygma* is not "pie in the sky by and by," a promise which rightfully wins communist scorn; it is heralding again and again the fact that "the unprecedented has happened; God has visited and redeemed his people."[7] It is proclaiming that we share in this redemption through baptism in which each of us is made "a member of Christ, the child of God, and an inheritor of the kingdom of heaven" (BCP, p. 283); it is setting forth the whole doctrine of God as revealed in the event of Christ to which the church's creeds witness.

Canon Max Warren has well pointed out: "The gospel is not good news about what our faith can enjoy. It is first of all and essentially good news about what God in his grace has done."[8] This preaching, still a sign that the age of fulfillment is come, must be in itself an experience whereby men are confronted with God, and brought into that new relationship with him, whereby we cry, "Abba, Father."

In a recent issue of the *Chaplain*, W. B. J. Martin says, "J. Middleton Murray once wrote, 'A truly great novel is a tale to the simple, a parable to the wise, and a direct revelation of reality to the man who has made it part of his being.' Is this not also true of sermons? When they are truly great they speak to more than one level of experience, and ultimately are more than vehicles for instruction, being events in which the congregation participates and through which it is illumined and enriched."[9]

This should be true not merely of our evangelistic missionary preaching but of the regular preaching to the faithful which is done as an essential part of the liturgy of the church. This Sunday by Sunday preaching, the sermon required by rubric in the Eucharist, as Dr. Fuller emphasizes in *What Is Liturgical Preaching?* corresponds to what is termed *paraklesis* in the New Testament, the effort to renew and deepen the faithful in their grasp of, and being grasped by the *kerygma*. The larger share of our normal Sunday preaching will be an effort to bring the converted and baptized through complete commitment, repentance, trust, obedience, and love to holiness. The aim of *kerygma* is to convert; of *paraklesis* to make saints of repentant and forgiven sinners, to bring Christian souls along the way of sanctification, to aid them in the steep ascent to heaven.

Our effort must be to make every public service of the church a unified experience for our people, by careful correlation of scripture, prayers, hymns, actions, sermon, in order to bring them into vital relationship with God in Christ through the inspiration of the Holy Spirit. Primarily we are concerned here with the Eucharist as the chief service, the definitive act of God's gathered people, his *ecclesia,* his holy church. Here word and sacrament are at one. With Fr. Bouyer we may say: "The whole eucharistic celebration is also a memorial. And here we must keep in mind a most important point . . . namely, that there is an inseparable connection between the two parts of the *synaxis,* that is, between the Bible readings and the meal. For the readings lead up to the meal. They recall to memory God's action of entering into the human history, redeeming it and fulfilling it from within; while the meal itself commemorates the climax of this process in the cross of Christ. And the meal needs the readings to point out to us the way to see it aright, not as a separate event of today, but understandable only in reference to a decisive action accomplished once and for all in the past. Such a consideration will bring us in due time to see that the whole Mass is a single liturgy of the Word, who began by speaking to man, who continues speaking to him more and more intimately; who finally spoke to him most directly in the Word-made-flesh; and who now speaks from the very heart of man himself to God the Father through the spirit."[10]

The liturgical sermon is an integral part of the reading of the Word and of the eucharistic action. It is not its primary purpose to explain the scripture lesson chosen by the church, or to relate the truth therein to the people's immediate situation, though it does both of these. Its primary purpose is "to relate the pericope to the *kerygma* which it proclaims and then link it up with the liturgical action which is to follow. His [the preacher's] first task is thus to penetrate behind the liturgical gospel to The Gospel, the *evangelion,* the proclamation of the central event of

Jesus Christ which it enshrines."[11] In preaching from the liturgical epistle, the task is the same. "If the epistle is taken from the doctrinal portion of the epistles the preacher's task will be to penetrate the doctrinal argumentation to the *kerygma* whose implications are being set forth, and to confront the congregation with that *kerygma* so that they might renew their response to it in faith preparatory to the Godward memorial of the liturgical action. And the epistle from the paraenetic sections will demand a similar treatment. . . . His [the preacher's] task is to penetrate behind the *parainesis* to the *kerygma* it presupposes, to confront the congregation with that *kerygma* so that it may be the occasion of a renewed encounter with Jesus Christ in the liturgy and thence to indicate the kind of behaviour that encounter will imply in the daily lives of people in their contemporary situation."[12]

Hence, the content of our liturgical preaching will be God's encounter with and relationship to man as it is related in the scripture, and as it is now experienced by man. It is not too much to say that such preaching should be a revelation of almighty God "as it was in the beginning, is now, and ever shall be, world without end. Amen." (BCP, p. 25) Now as in that century long since past, he should dwell among us, and men should behold "his glory, the glory as of the only begotten of the Father, full of grace and truth." (Jn. 1:14)

Now we cannot limit the definition of Christian

preaching only to *kerygma,* the proclamation of the Good News of salvation wrought in Christ. Preaching must also include elucidation of that faith and teaching of its doctrinal and ethical implications, that is, both *paraklesis* and *didache;* and it must do so for two reasons. First, I am not convinced that preaching in the primitive church was limited to *kerygma* in spite of the distinction of the threefold ministry of the Word in the New Testament. In this, I am in agreement with John Knox of Union Theological Seminary, who raises the same question.[13] Secondly, as a practical matter, if sermons to the faithful gathered for public worship do not ever teach, the faithful will continue to be religiously illiterate, for the pulpit presents the one continuing opportunity that the church has to teach.

Hence, I would insist that at Morning and Evening Prayer on Sunday, at Lenten services, and the like, normally the sermon should teach. With Fr. Bull, we may distinguish three fields for Christian teaching: dogmatics, ethics, and exposition of the scripture.[14] Preaching dogmatics is preaching Christ as the way, the truth, and the life. We must teach the discipline of the Christian life, the way of salvation; the doctrine of the Christian religion, the fullness of our faith; the sacramental life of the Christian Church, the means of grace. In seeking to help our people understand the religion which they profess, we must hold Christ up before them as the way, the truth, in order that they may find in him the more abundant, eternal life.

Christian ethics, we must teach, is the expression of the Christian's vocation to love God and to love man. Our effort is to bring to the souls committed to our charge the understanding envisioned by Dr. Dodd, "Christian morality consists in giving effect in human relations to the divine charity which is the glory of God disclosed in the work of Christ."[15] In this we are seeking to move our people to higher moral endeavor, to goodness, to holiness, "unto a perfect man, unto the measure of the stature of the fulness of Christ." (Eph. 4:13)

Our preaching must be expository, setting forth the words of life; explaining, expounding, exhorting in terms and language that our people can understand, that through their apprehension of the Life therein revealed, they may have life, abundant and eternal. In such sermons we must strive to make our preaching God's answer (in part at least) to his faithful people's prayer: "Blessed Lord, who hast caused all holy Scriptures to be written for our learning; Grant that we may in such wise hear them, read, mark, learn, and inwardly digest them, that by patience and comfort of thy holy Word, we may embrace, and ever hold fast, the blessed hope of everlasting life, which thou hast given us in our Saviour Jesus Christ. *Amen.*" (BCP, p. 92)

In all of this *didache,* the content of our preaching seeks to present the answer to man's perennial desire uttered by those ancient Greeks who came to worship at the feast, "Sir, we would see Jesus." (Jn. 12:21) The content is him of whom St. Peter testified, "Lord, to whom shall we go? thou hast the words of eternal life." (Jn. 6:68)

The scripture, then, is the content of our preaching: "For whatsoever things were written aforetime were written for our learning, that we through patience and comfort of the scriptures might have hope. Now the God of patience and consolation grant you to be likeminded one toward another according to Christ Jesus: That ye may with one mind and one mouth glorify God, even the Father of our Lord Jesus Christ." (Rom. 15:4–6)

4

Some Reflections on Method in Preaching

To DISCUSS the method of preaching is to seek an answer to the question, "How are we commanded to preach?" or, in other words, to discuss the preparation, composition, and delivery of a sermon. To preach any sermon successfully, three fundamental principles must be observed. The preacher must have something worth while to say or he is wasting his and the congregation's time. He must express his thinking clearly and in an interesting manner if those in the pews are to listen and to hear what is being said. And the sermon must be delivered effectively to move the hearts and minds and wills of men. Of these three, the first, having something of value to say, is of supreme importance. The latter two, expression and delivery, though cast in supporting roles, make or break the sermon.

Once again it is the part of wisdom to examine first the preaching of our Lord and of the Apostles in the New Testament, granting that we have only circumstantial, not direct evidence concerning the preparation, composition, and delivery of those sermons.

One observation that can be made about the preparation of our Lord and the Apostles for their preaching is that they thoroughly grounded their thought in the scriptures of Israel. One need only glance at the cross-references in any student's Bible to realize how frequently they quote from, refer to, or base their teaching on those scriptures. St. Paul's question, "What sayeth the scripture?" (Rom. 4:3) well describes the starting place of all New Testament teaching and preaching. What he says of Timothy, "From a child thou hast known the holy scriptures, which are able to make thee wise unto salvation" (II Tim. 3:15), might just as truly be said of our Lord and those he sent forth to speak in his name.

Already have we indicated that Jesus was the master storyteller. He speaks with the utmost simplicity, clarity, and with an economy of words that all preachers would do well to emulate. By parable, figure of speech, and analogy, he brings his teaching home to men. Immediately there spring to mind the parables of the Good Samaritan, the Prodigal Son, the Wicked Husbandman; or the picturesque figure, "It is easier for a camel to go through the eye of a needle, than for a rich man to enter into the kingdom of God" (Mk. 10:25); or the analogy in which he likens the kingdom of heaven to a grain of mustard seed, to leaven, to treasure hid in a field. This ability to present general truths by vivid illustrations, to portray the abstract in the concrete, is, of course, literary skill of the highest order. Moreover, teaching in such form can be apprehended by every man.

The Apostles' sermons are found in the book of Acts, though their preaching is also reflected in the gospels and the Epistle to the Hebrews. The evidence of both the book of Acts and the gospels suggests a similar simplicity, clarity, and economy of words. The Epistle to the Hebrews, which is *paraklesis* rather than *kerygma,* is of necessity reasoned argument of greater length. But all the evidence indicates that apostolic preaching was brief, direct, and straightforward, not prolix and involved. One exception to this brevity is the account of St. Paul's preaching at Troas where he "continued his speech until midnight." But be it noted that "as Paul was long preaching, [Eutychus] sank down with sleep." (Acts 20:7, 9) In this, we should do well not to emulate the greatest evangelist the world has ever known.

Although we have no precise description concerning the style of delivery used either by our Lord or the early Christian preachers, certain observations can be made. Apparently, he frequently spoke to crowds even while seated. The Sermon on the Mount is introduced by the statement, "And seeing the multitudes, he went up into a mountain: and when he was set, his disciples came unto him." (Matt. 5:1) In the Gospel according to St. Luke, these same sayings are delivered as he stands in the plain. When arrested in the garden he speaks, "Are ye come out as against a thief with swords and staves for to take me? I sat daily with you teaching in the temple, and ye laid no hold on me." (Matt. 26:55) St. Mark tells us that because of the multitude on one occasion, "he entered into a ship, and sat in the sea" (4:1); and taught those on the shore. His informal posture would seem to indicate that his delivery was informally conversational. Such a conjecture is supported by the literary style of his reported utterances.

It is interesting to note in passing that Dr. Broadus asserts that the Greek *homilia* (the root of our word "homiletics") signifies conversation, mutual talk; hence, familiar discourse. Of this, we are not sure because the word also means "assembly." The Latin *sermo*, however, whence comes "sermon," has also the sense of conversation, talk, and discussion.[1]

Be that as it may, talking as our Lord did to multitudes numbering in the thousands, he must have spoken at such times with appreciable force. Surely the astonishment of the people that he spoke "as one having authority" (Matt. 7:29) reflects the delivery as well as the content of his teaching. On the other hand, the settings as well as the context of the few sermons in the book of Acts indicate formal, forceful preaching aimed at convincing the hearers. Not only the three thousand baptized on Pentecost, but the rapid growth of the early church, all on the basis of conversion, evidence that the Apostles spoke with power both as to content and delivery.

Preaching demands, as does any art, a lifetime of preparation. If truth is to be presented from the pulpit for the minds of the hearers to grasp, hard and systematic thinking must go into the preparation. For this reason the church normally requires both college and seminary education of those whom we ordain to preach. And all our learning and all that we can learn is of practical value in sermon preparation. We must strive to develop what might be termed a homiletical eye and ear.

It is not given to every man to be an outstanding preacher but any man can be a better preacher than he is, if he is willing to work at it. Preaching has fallen to a low estate among us because many clergymen—and I have known them—do not regard their sermon as a God-given opportunity to change men's lives. Instead, week after week, they prepare for the pulpit by jotting down a few points on a scrap of paper between church school and eleven o'clock Sunday morning or compose their message sitting in an easy chair in the living room on Saturday night after dinner or frantically search around for something to say on Friday or Saturday.

Sermons hold interest and enlighten by the use of illustrations which throw light upon the truth presented. Common sense suggests the use of stories and illustrations to capture the attention and engage the imagination. In this as in all things our Lord is master. But always it must be remembered that these devices are meant to illuminate, not amuse and entertain. So-called "popular" preaching presents its points step by step, as if building a house, but too often paint is substituted for studding! Humor in preaching is certainly permissible, but the pulpit comedian with his store of funny stories normally offers little competition to Bob Hope and Jack Benny and the laughter may be "at" rather than "with."

Pathetic is the preacher who is a disciple of the 1,001 sermon illustrations. Such highly artificial means of catching interest can sometimes get by with the kindergarten or lower-grade folk but inevitably bore adults. The preacher who uses frequent personal anecdotes in his sermons, even when he does not betray confidences, tends to stretch the truth—and thus casts doubt on his own integrity.

Members of the school of copious and learned quotations impress few others than themselves. Most members of your congregation really will not be awed by the fact that you casually mention Barth, Brunner, Bultmann; to them, Tillich and Kierkegaard will sound strangely foreign. We must learn from these great thinkers of our time, but the verb is "learn," not make a card index of apt quotations to awe the rustics.

On the other hand, our people will know and consider as old friends, Matthew, Mark, Luke, and John, Paul, James, and Peter, to say nothing of the stalwarts of the Old Testament, Moses, David, Isaiah, Jeremiah, and the rest. And they should come increasingly to know our Lord. If not, our preaching is a total failure.

The source of illustrations is myriad; our knowledge of literature, history, art, science is of real use here. It is difficult to think of a single subject studied or a single book read that does not offer some illustrative material that sooner or later can be used. This is not to say that notes taken on seminary lectures make good sermons, as many a mission congregation can testify.

If we are to fulfill our priestly calling to be mediators between God and man, we must know both God and man. The former knowledge should result from our practice of religion, our devotional life, our worship. The latter knowledge comes in part from education in history, literature, psychology, the social sciences, and the like. In larger part it springs from being faithful pastors to our people. One can be a good pastor—knowing, being concerned about, and loving the members of the flock—without being a good preacher. It is doubtful if one can ever become a really good preacher without the background knowledge that being a faithful pastor brings.

Every personal experience offers to the preacher an opportunity to gather illustrative materials. In this we ought to follow the example of Jesus, who taught tellingly by reference to the poor woman who lost a coin, to the flower in the field, to bread rising. His use of homely, practical, everyday experience, known and shared by those who heard, is truth communication at its best.

Many years ago Charles Henry Brent, under whom I became a postulant for Holy Orders, suggested that since no man could possibly read the vast flood of Christian literature pouring forth from the presses, and since so very much would prove hardly worth reading in any case, it would be of greater value by far to master four or five great books a year than to gallop through the unceasing stream of books written for popular consumption. St. Augustine, St. Thomas Aquinas, Richard Hooker, spring to mind, but the counsel is not merely to read ancient authors. Modern works have value too. For example, in the art of homiletics, every priest who intends to obey the command to preach should, in my opinion, not only read but know St. Augustine's *Christian Instruction,* C. H. Dodd's *Apostolic Preaching,* Reginald H. Fuller's *What Is Liturgical Preaching?* Easton and Robbins' *The Eternal Word in the Modern World, Preaching the Christian Year* edited by Howard A. Johnson, Massey H. Shepherd's *The Oxford American Prayer Book Commentary,* and of course, *The Interpreter's Bible.*

Above all, we who are commanded to preach must hear, read, mark, learn, and inwardly digest the Holy Scriptures. Only by studying the scriptures, and meditating thereon, can we insure that we stand in the long line of those who dare proclaim, "Thus saith the Lord." When we speak with such assurance we should stand ready with an answer to the fair question any of our folk may ask us, "In what book, chapter, and verse may that be found?" In passing, we should also be warned that when we say, "The church teaches" we should be prepared to give the reference to the scripture or the Book of Common Prayer.

Because of this, I dare make two practical suggestions. All of us must strive for faithfulness in the daily recitation of the offices of Morning and Evening Prayer. Thus we pray with the church, and thus we insure daily reading from the Bible. We must, moreover, work out some plan for reading and rereading the Holy Scriptures in their entirety. I learned in the army that, by reading ten to twelve chapters a day, the New Testament could be read through each month, and I did just that until I was reasonably familiar with it. Now, I reread the New Testament each Lent by reading eight or nine chapters a day. I find it helpful to read each Lent a different translation, from J. B. Phillips to the Douay Version. I read, in order, Matthew, Hebrews, James; Mark and Peter; Luke, Acts, St. Paul's epistles; the Johannine gospel, epistles and Revelation.

To read and reread the Old Testament and the Apocrypha takes more time. The former takes, using the same system, about three months; it can usually be read in the period from the Feast of the Circumcision to Easter. The Apocrypha is much shorter; reading in it about twenty or thirty minutes a day, one can finish it in about three weeks—during the pre-Lenten season, for example. How else could our time be better spent?

Merely reading and rereading the Bible is, of course, not an end in itself. St. Augustine pointed out long ago: "Furthermore, a man speaks more or less wisely in proportion as he has made more or less progress in the Holy Scriptures. I do not mean in the extensive reading and memorizing of them, but in a thorough understanding and careful searching into their meanings."[2]

St. Augustine compares the man who memorizes and does not understand to the one who sees "with the eyes of his heart the soul of scripture"; he finds the latter preferable by far. He then goes on to say, "But, better than either of these is the man who, when he wishes, both cites scripture and understands it as he should." At least one other point he makes that all who preach should remember, "It is particularly essential for the man who should say with wisdom even what he cannot say eloquently to remember (and quote) the words of scripture."[3]

In calling your attention to these words of St. Augustine, I do not mean to imply that the art of preaching is an intellectual attainment, although God has given us brains and we are supposed to use them. Need the obvious be said? A man cannot convey religion unless he has it.

Normally, the Holy Spirit does not use the unconverted as an instrument of conversion. If we are not committed, we can scarcely hope to bring men to complete commitment. How can the unrepentant (and we are all sinners) demand a response of repentance? the disobedient, obedience? the nonbelieving, belief? the unfaithful, faith? the fearful, trust? Dare we hope to bring our people to love God and man if we ourselves are lacking in love? It is wise to remember Bishop Brent's counsel to his clergy: "Today what we clergy must make our own is righteousness. It is the only proof that Christ is and is here."[4]

To tell the old, old story of Jesus and his love is part of the presentation of the Gospel, but it is hardly more relevant than other tales from ancient history unless we can testify with St. Paul, "For the love of Christ constraineth us." (II Cor. 5:14) How can God reveal himself through us save as Christ dwells in our "hearts by faith" (Eph. 3:17); unless we know ourselves increasingly to be temples of the Holy Spirit; except daily we walk with God?

Only on such a foundation of continued preparation can we build by immediate preparation sermons that have something of real worth to say. The first step in the immediate preparation of a sermon is: to be certain of our aim, our understanding, and our attitude. The purpose of a sermon is not to impress the congregation with our ability, our learning, or our zeal. It has been wisely said, "No man can at the same time persuade an audience that he is clever and that Jesus is the Christ."[5] Nowhere is St. Paul's admonition, "whatsoever ye do, do all to the glory of God" (I Cor. 10:31), more pertinent than in the making of sermons.

We hear much in the church these days of stewardship, that we offer to God a fair share of our time, ability, and possessions in token that all things come of him. Look then on each sermon as an offering, a sacrifice to him. Think of it not as words but as action, not merely saying something but doing something. We speak much of the mighty acts of God. Pray to him that each sermon we preach may be one of his minor acts at least.

Denis Baly has shrewdly observed that much of the present weakness in preaching comes "from the incorrigible tendency of clergy to visualize their congregations as the ultimate recipients of their teaching." He then goes on to say: "To preach the word is so to labor, in the pulpit and out of it, that it may be a living thing among the people, and may both return with power from them to the priest, for the health and benefit of his soul, and go forth from the people of God to the world."[6]

Accordingly, in the art of preaching as in all else we can depend on God. "The assurance about God will be an assurance about God's own activity. As God moved first in regard to the evangelist so it will be assumed that God has moved first with regard to those to whom the evangelist goes."[7]

The second step in immediate preparation of the sermon is prayer. "Pray without ceasing" (I Thess. 5:17), says Paul, echoing our Lord's teaching in the parable of the Unjust Judge, "that men ought always to pray, and not to faint." (Lk. 18:1) Pray for the guidance of the Holy Spirit as you begin your preparation. Make the effort itself a prayer. Pray for his blessing as you enter the pulpit that he may accept and use your offering. Before the service ends, ask his forgiveness that your preaching was so inadequate, so unworthy of his glory. As in formal meditation, we can trust the Holy Spirit to guide our thinking in the work of sermon construction, if we will truly think and make of that thinking real prayer in God's own presence.

The third step in composing a sermon is studying the scriptures. The classical definition of sermons, as textual, expository, or topical, is, in my opinion, of minor value. Topical or subject sermons that cannot be grounded in the scriptures we have no business preaching. Surely in the little pulpit time we have, our primary emphasis must be on man's salvation.

Having the great advantage of the Christian year, normally we start with the lessons appointed for that day and service. In this way we are assured that we shall present to our people the whole gospel of God and may one day be able to say with the Apostle at Ephesus, "For I have not shunned to declare unto you all the counsel of God." (Acts 20:27) Your choice of text need not be limited to the stated lessons, of course, but the connection between what the church wants taught on a particular occasion and what we ministers of the church teach on that day or season should be abundantly plain. In preaching from the scripture, observe three rules. Understand the verse or passage in its context, interpret it in accordance with its given meaning (given by the author and the setting), and expound it in accordance with and not contrary to the general teaching of the scriptures. It is here that commentaries are an invaluable, yes, indispensable tool.

The methods of constructing, composing, writing

sermons are many and varied. Ultimately each of us must work out the system that suits him best. Dr. Robert J. McCracken of the Riverside Church in New York City describes Frederick W. Norwood's method of composing his great extemporaneous sermons: "Norwood told me that when he had fixed on a subject he would lie down on a sofa and let his mind go to work on the subject. One by one ideas would suggest themselves to him and he would proceed to sort them out in sequence. Gradually the sermon outline would begin to take form. . . . It was his contention that if ideas are clear in the mind, and a man has a reasonable facility of speech, he will have no problem in the matter of expression. He will have no need even to jot down heads or divisions. The structure and sequence will stand out in the memory."[8]

That was fine for Norwood. Most extemporaneous preachers unfortunately keep on talking while they are trying to think of what next to say. Two good preachers I have known well prided themselves on writing nothing. They had something of value to say, they expressed it clearly and held the interest of the congregation, and they spoke convincingly. But, in the long last, the method failed. In both instances, faithful members of their respective congregations complained that these preachers constantly repeated themselves.

To write out our sermons is a reasonable guarantee that we shall not repeat ourselves unwittingly. By use of simple notations with a file of written sermons we can know exactly what we have said and where we have said it. There is much kidding about the preacher's proverbial barrel of sermons, but such a file is invaluable if we abide by one basic rule: never repreach a sermon without reworking it. And surely, it can stand improvement.

The real advantages of writing out the sermon lie in the development of style through word choice and sentence structure, the orderly and logical sequence of thought, and conciseness of expression. In passing, remember that simplicity of diction is the ultimate rule of eloquence.

A word must be said about vocabulary. Somehow the foolish notion has been noised abroad that since our hearers today for the most part do not understand the great words of the Christian faith—Incarnation, Redemption, Atonement, Justification, Grace, and the like—then the Gospel must be presented in modern garb and in the language of the street. Nonsense! If our people do not understand, it is our task to teach them. It would be just as sensible to say that to teach trigonometry one must find an everyday synonym for sine, cosine, and coefficient as those terms are not understood by the ones who seek to learn. In teaching, a basic rule is repetition. We should use the Christian vocabulary presenting the Christian faith but always and without fail immediately define our terms in words the learner may understand more easily. For example, when referring to the Incarnation, speak of the fact that God's only begotten Son took our flesh upon him and dwelt on this earth as man.

Reasonable brevity is of tremendous importance in spite of P. T. Forsyth's argument to the contrary.[9] The attention span of the average person is not long; in all probability what is said after twenty to thirty minutes might as well be left unsaid. It takes hard work to say in 20 minutes what it is needful to say, but it is worth the effort. Better psychologically and spiritually to have people say, "He stopped too soon," than, "I thought he was never going to quit." Bishop Wing used to say, "It is not given to every man to be a brilliant preacher, but no man needs to be long-winded. To bore briefly is forgivable, to bore at length is deadly."

Eloquence comes normally from hard work before we enter the pulpit and it is a value to be cultivated. Hear St. Augustine: "The power of eloquence—so very effective in convincing us of either wrong or right—lies open to all. Why, then, do not the good zealously procure it that it may serve truth, if the wicked, in order to gain unjustifiable and groundless cases, apply it to the advantages of injustice and error?"[10] He goes on to quote with favor Cicero, "An eloquent man should speak in such a way that he 'teaches, pleases, and persuades'. . . . to teach is a necessity, to please is a satisfaction, and to persuade is a triumph."[11] To teach is to be understood; to please is to keep our hearers listening; and to persuade obviously influences men to act. The first depends upon what we say, the latter two on how we say it, —expression and delivery.

Quite as important as writing is outlining. An outline is the necessary skeleton to give the body form; hence, it is essential for all good writing and all good preaching. Thirty years ago over the radio I heard Harry Emerson Fosdick preach on pain, a sermon I still remember. He dealt with the various attitudes with which men face the fact of suffering in human life and contrasted the attitudes of the defeated and the stoic with that of the Christian who, after the example of his crucified Master, sees in pain the instrument of redemption and the means to victory.

Personally, I usually use the traditional three point sermon, trying to remember not to take detours but to hew only to those points, major and minor, that are germane and necessary to accomplish the sermon's aim and purpose. For each of the three major points, the emphasis is apt to be different. The introduction and conclusion are more difficult to compose. Both should be brief. The introduction must be geared to enlist attention immediately. The conclusion, which hearers remember easily, must drive home the message of the sermon. It should challenge a response.

Cicero's rules of rhetoric quoted in *Christian Instruction* apply both to style of language and manner of delivery, "He will be eloquent, then, who can speak about trivial subjects in a subdued style, ordinary subjects in a moderate style, and noble subjects in a grand style." St. Augustine further elucidates, "He will be eloquent, then, who, in order to teach, can speak about trivial subjects in a subdued style; in order to please can discuss ordinary subjects in a moderate style; and in order to persuade, can treat of noble subjects in a grand style."[12]

The change of pace guaranteed by being guided by these rules of rhetoric will aid much in holding interest as we preach. The test of good delivery, however, lies in believing that what we say is of great importance, and in acting that way. Broadus quotes with approval Cardinal Newman's advice in his *University Preaching*: "Talent, logic, learning, words, manner, voice, action, all are required for the perfection of a preacher; but 'one thing is necessary'—an intense perception and appreciation of the end for which he preaches, and that is, to be the minister of some definite spiritual good to those who hear him. . . . I do not mean that a preacher must aim at earnestness, but he must aim at his object, which is to do some spiritual good to his hearers, and which will at once make him earnest."[13] Preaching to the whole man—mind, heart, and will—we must preach with the whole man. The unmoved preacher will not move others. Reason supports, but emotion fires the will. This is not a plea for emotionalism, but for emotion in preaching.

It is far easier to do this when one is not restricted by manuscript nor hampered by notes. We hasten to add that many excellent preachers use both. If we forget a point, it is not important, provided the whole makes sense. As a matter of fact, only we are conscious of the omission. A word of caution, one does sometimes fail to remember a point. Preaching at the consecration of the present Bishop of Atlanta, I said, "Three things must be remembered. One . . ., two. . . ." and "three" disappeared in the deep recesses of memory for the moment. Since then, I do not advertise my enumeration.

At the General Convention in Boston, the House of Bishops was addressed by the then primate of the Anglican Church in Canada, the Most Rev. Walter Foster Barfoot. He spoke simply of the Church in Canada, its problems and its opportunities, its successes and its failures. In closing his informal address, he said, "As a matter of fact, the only religious bodies in Canada which are really growing are the Roman Catholic Church and the Pentecostal and Holiness sects because they believe that what they are doing matters eternally." Do we believe that what we do in obedience to his command to preach matters eternally? Pray God, we must believe it lest we be totally unworthy servants.

"Eye hath not seen, nor ear heard, neither have entered into the heart of man, the things which God hath prepared for them that love him." (I Cor. 2:9) By preaching we show forth our love for him, seeking a response of love, that he may be everywhere and forever glorified.

Cleanse my heart and my lips, O Almighty God, who didst purge the lips of the prophet Isaiah with a live coal: and of thy gracious mercy, vouchsafe so to purify me, that I may worthily proclaim Thy Holy Gospel; through Christ our Lord. Amen.[14]

Notes

1. "Commanded To Preach"

1. *Christian Century*, LXXVII, January 20, 1960, p. 71.
2. Reginald H. Fuller, *What Is Liturgical Preaching?* p. 53.
3. Paul B. Bull, *Preaching and Sermon Construction*, p. 40.
4. Gregory Dix, *The Shape of the Liturgy*, p. 40.
5. Paul B. Bull, *ibid.*, p. 39.
6. *Ibid.*, p. 1.
7. Louis Bouyer, *Liturgical Piety*, p. 148.
8. Canon 50, On Lay Readers, Sec. 3 (6), p. 133.

2. The Purpose of Preaching

1. Reginald H. Fuller, *What Is Liturgical Preaching?* p. 53.
2. Dr. John A. Broadus wrote long ago, "Preaching is characteristic of Christianity. No false religion has ever provided for the regular and frequent assemblies of men to have religious instruction and exhortation." From *The Preparation and Delivery of Sermons*, p. 17.
3. Ernest F. Scott, *The Kingdom of God in the New Testament*, quoted in *The Interpreter's Bible*, VII, 656.
4. Alan Richardson, *The Theology of the New Testament*, p. 30.
5. C. H. Dodd, *The Apostolic Preaching*, p. 9.
6. Phillips Brooks, *On Preaching*, pp. 5, 21, 32.
7. Paul B. Bull, *Preaching and Sermon Construction*, pp. 51–2.
8. Reginald H. Fuller, *ibid.*, p. 12.
9. William Temple, *Towards the Conversion of England*, p. 1.
10. Reginald H. Fuller, *ibid.*, p. 21.
11. *Ibid.*, p. 22.
12. *Ibid.*, p. 21.

13. Louis Bouyer, *Liturgical Piety*, p. 29.
14. Max Warren, *Challenge and Response*, p. 69.

3. THE CONTENT OF PREACHING

1. Samuel M. Shoemaker, *With the Holy Spirit and with Fire*, p. 49.
2. Phillips Brooks, *On Preaching*, p. 129.
3. C. H. Dodd, *The Apostolic Preaching*, p. 21.
4. *Ibid.*, p. 76.
5. Reginald H. Fuller, *What Is Liturgical Preaching?* p. 22.
6. Constitution, Protestant Episcopal Church in U.S.A., Article VIII.
7. C. H. Dodd, *ibid.*, p. 33.
8. Max Warren, *Challenge and Response*, p. 53.
9. *Chaplain*, XVII, August, 1960, p. 21.
10. Louis Bouyer, *Liturgical Piety*, p. 79.
11. Reginald H. Fuller, *ibid.*, p. 37.
12. *Ibid.*, p. 25.
13. John Knox, *The Integrity of Preaching*, p. 49.
14. Paul B. Bull, *Preaching and Sermon Construction*, p. 10.
15. C. H. Dodd, *ibid.*, p. 25.

4. SOME REFLECTIONS ON METHOD IN PREACHING

1. John A. Broadus, *The Preparation and Delivery of Sermons*, p. 4.
2. St. Augustine, *Christian Instruction*, p. 173.
3. *Ibid.*, p. 174.
4. *Chaplain*, XVII, June, 1960, p. 8.
5. *Christianity Today*, IV, August 29, 1960, p. 52.
6. *Bulletin* (Bexley Hall, Kenyon College, Gambier, Ohio), September–October, 1959.
7. Max Warren, *Challenge and Response*, p. 55.
8. Robert J. McCracken, *The Making of the Sermon*, p. 66.
9. P. T. Forsyth, *Positive Preaching and the Modern Mind*, p. 75.
10. St. Augustine, *ibid.*, p. 169.
11. *Ibid.*, p. 193.
12. *Ibid.*, p. 201.
13. John A. Broadus, *ibid.*, p. 237.
14. Anglican Missal, "Prayers before the Holy Gospel."

Bibliography

Augustine, Saint. *Writings.* IV. *Christian Instruction.* New York: Fathers of the Church, Inc., 1950.

Bouyer, Louis. *Liturgical Piety.* Indiana: University of Notre Dame Press, 1955.

Broadus, John A. *The Preparation and Delivery of Sermons.* New York: A. C. Armstrong & Son, 1896.

Brooks, Phillips. *On Preaching.* New York: Seabury Press, 1964.

Brown, Charles Reynolds. *The Art of Preaching.* New York: Macmillan Co., 1940.

Bull, Paul B. *Preaching and Sermon Construction.* New York: Macmillan Co., 1922.

Buttrick, George A. *Jesus Came Preaching.* New York: Charles Scribner's Sons, 1931.

Caemmerer, Richard R. *Preaching to the Church.* St. Louis, Missouri: Concordia Publishing House, 1959.

Coffin, Henry Sloane. *Communion Through Preaching.* New York: Charles Scribner's Sons, 1952.

de Dietrich, Suzanne. *The Witnessing Community.* Philadelphia: The Westminster Press, 1958.

Dix, Gregory. *The Shape of the Liturgy.* London: Dacre Press, 1945.

Dodd, C. H. *The Apostolic Preaching.* New York: Harper & Row, 1955.

Ferris, Theodore Parker. *Go Tell the People.* New York: Charles Scribner's Sons, 1951.

Fisk, Franklin W. *Manual of Preaching.* New York: A. C. Armstrong & Son, 1904.

Forsyth, P. T. *Positive Preaching and the Modern Mind.* London: Independent Press, 1957.

Fuller, Reginald H. *What Is Liturgical Preaching?* Naperville, Illinois: Alec R. Allenson, Inc., 1957.

Garrison, Webb B. *The Preacher and His Audience.* London: Fleming H. Revell Co., 1954.

Hart, A. Tindal. *The Country Priest in English History.* London: Phoenix House, 1959.

Hough, Lynn Harold. *The Living Church.* St. Louis, Missouri: The Bethany Press, 1959.

The Interpreter's Bible. Nashville, Tenn.: Abingdon Press, 1962.

Ireson, Gordon W. *How Shall They Hear?* London: SPCK (The Society for Promoting Christian Knowledge), 1958.

Johnson, Howard A., editor. *Preaching the Christian Year.* New York: Charles Scribner's Sons, 1957.

Knox, John. *The Integrity of Preaching.* Nashville, Tenn.: Abingdon Press, 1957.

Luccock, Helforde. *In the Minister's Workshop.* Nashville, Tenn.: Abingdon Press, 1944.

MacLennan, David A. *Entrusted with the Gospel.* Philadelphia: Westminster Press, 1956.

McCracken, Robert J. *The Making of the Sermon.* New York: Harper & Row, 1956.

Morris, Frederick M. *Preach the Word of God.* New York: Morehouse-Barlow Co., 1954.

Nes, William H. *The Excellency of the Word.* New York: Morehouse-Barlow Co., 1956.

Niles, D. T. *The Preacher's Task and the Stone of Stumbling.* New York: Harper & Row, 1958.

Pearson, Roy. *The Ministry of Preaching.* New York: Harper & Row, 1959.

Richardson, Alan. *The Theology of the New Testament.* New York: Harper & Row, 1958.

Shepherd, Massey H., Jr. *The Oxford American Prayer Book Commentary.* New York: Oxford University Press, 1950.

Shoemaker, Samuel M. *With the Holy Spirit and with Fire.* New York: Harper & Row, 1960.

Smith, Roland Cotton. *Preaching as a Fine Art.* New York: Macmillan Co., 1922.

Smith, W. Spooner. *Sermon Reading.* Boston: The Gorham Press, 1916.

Temple, William. *Towards the Conversion of England.* Westminster, England: Press and Publications Board of the Church Assembly, 1945.

Von Allmen, J. J., editor. *Companion to the Bible.* New York: Oxford University Press, 1958.

Warren, Max. *Challenge and Response.* New York: Morehouse-Barlow Co., 1959.